SYNANON KID

A MEMOIR OF GROWING UP IN THE SYNANON CULT

C.A. WITTMAN

Copyright © 2017 by C.A. Wittman

All rights reserved.

No part of this book may be reproduced in any form or by any electronic or mechanical means, including information storage and retrieval systems, without written permission from the author, except for the use of brief quotations in a book review.

❊ Created with Vellum

For my Mother

CONTENTS

Prologue	1
Chapter 1	3
Chapter 2	13
Chapter 3	17
Chapter 4	22
Chapter 5	32
Chapter 6	37
Chapter 7	41
Chapter 8	56
Chapter 9	61
Chapter 10	66
Chapter 11	72
Chapter 12	81
Chapter 13	85
Chapter 14	92
Chapter 15	98
Chapter 16	114
Chapter 17	124
Chapter 18	129
Chapter 19	142
Chapter 20	145
Chapter 21	152
Chapter 22	157
Chapter 23	166
Chapter 24	177
Chapter 25	193
Chapter 26	199
Chapter 27	204
Chapter 28	213
Chapter 29	221
Chapter 30	228

Chapter 31	246
Chapter 32	253
A Short History of Synanon	258
Acknowledgments	263
About the Author	267

PROLOGUE

Childhood is convalescence from being dead for all eternity and should therefore be gotten over as quickly as possible.

—CED (Charles Edward Dederich, founder of Synanon)

NATURE ROOTS herself firmly in my childhood memories of Synanon. Rustling hills of tall blond grass scenting the air with subtle sweetness. An afternoon picking blackberries, so many that crimson juice stains my hands, face and clothes, the sticky residue gumming up between my fingers. My dark, sun-kissed skin muddied with Indian red.

The creek, a wide rushing torrent of water taking all in its path, roars out a warning of danger. In the summer, deep, still pools, afterthoughts of brisk winter business left scattered along the banks, invite a swim, that first dip so cold it chokes the breath.

The people are secondary, melding into the background; forgettable adults, their features wiped clean in my mind of any defining characteristics. Some stand out, the cruelest ones; the mean, unwanted children housed in bland dormitories, and the sterile "demonstrators." Hate is a feeling to curl up with, a comfort in the sort of childhood that one longs to shuck off as quickly as possible.

CHAPTER ONE

I nduction

IT WAS EVENING when I arrived at Synanon with my mother and her friend Mary Ann. I was six years old and tired from the long bus ride. Having lived all my life in South Central Los Angeles, I found nothing familiar in the country environment in which I found myself. It seemed as though I'd left somewhere and arrived at a place that felt like nowhere.

No one greeted us. After we retrieved our minimal luggage, we walked in silence along a gravel road devoid of cars, the small stones crunching beneath our shoes. A sheet of white clouds covered the sky, lending an austere, colorless look to the shed-like structures that hunkered down on the dusky land. Within minutes we traversed the buildings, the road snaking through a natural setting. Dry, brittle-looking hills sprouting mushrooms of stunted, tightly clustered trees ringed the property.

My mother, whose hand I held, was nearly a stranger to me. I had not seen her in more than two years; yet within the last twenty-four hours, she and Mary Ann had whisked me away in the night from my uncle's home, where I'd been visiting. The three of us had spent the night in a rundown hotel in Santa Monica, California. In the early morning, we'd boarded a Greyhound-style bus called a Synacruiser bound for Marin, California, and the place called Synanon of which my mother had spoken.

As we rounded a bend in the country road, a two-story building with a metal roof came into view. I tightened my grip on my mother's hand. The building was still under construction. A new section had been added, though it was still just a hollow frame of wood. Other, similar structures fanned out, creating a cluster of dwellings. Without knocking, we went into one and walked along a short hallway to a living room, unfurnished except for a few good-sized beanbag chairs.

Eight or nine children and two women sat on the floor with their legs crossed. Like identical paper cutouts, each of the children and the women were as bald as the next and dressed exactly the same, in overalls. Expectation seemed to crackle in the air, settling in gazes that became attentive and slumping shoulders that straightened as we came in.

One of the children stood, walked over to me and without a word reached out a hand to touch my hair. I pulled back, but my mother gently prodded me forward. I remained still, allowing the child to stroke my hair. The others rose up, one by one. Crowding around me, they reached out their hands to touch and pet my head. Someone grabbed tightly at my hair, yanking my head back.

I tried to pull away, feeling fear for the first time.

An adult, one of the children's supervisors, came to my rescue, pushing through the cluster of small bodies, separating them and swatting down their small hands.

"Behave," she said. "If you want to touch Celena's hair, you must stand in line. Everyone will get a chance."

I didn't want a group of strange kids stroking my head, but no one asked me or seemed to care what I thought. The odd-looking children, some of them sulking at the new arrangement, obediently formed a line.

My mother handed a hairbrush to the child nearest to me, the brush ready in her purse, though she was as bald as the others.

Wielding the prized tool, the child raked the bristles through my tresses, not at all like the soft motions of my mother's hand. On the bus ride to Marin, she had unbraided and combed through my hair several times while I ate endless slices of carrot-raisin bread. I braced myself for some seconds until the brushing abruptly halted in mid-stroke as the supervisor put an end to the activity by taking hold of the child's arm. "That's enough. Give it to Becky now." The ritual continued until each of the alien-looking children had a turn, touching me and brushing my hair as if I were a possession. My mother and her friend smiled approvingly. When it was over, my mother said, "I have to go now. I'll be back later."

Until that moment, I had taken the situation in stride with my mother near me, her presence a lifeline to the real world we had left behind and to which I was sure I'd return. It had not occurred to me that I would be left with these people. I grabbed the lower fringe of her jacket. "Where are you going?"

She removed my hands, and a flutter of panic rose in my chest.

"It's a surprise," she said.

I'd had enough surprises. My muscles tensed as she turned toward the hallway with Mary Ann behind her. I heard the door open, then click shut as they walked out, leaving me with the strangers who openly stared at me in my too-bright clothes with my big puffy hair fanning out around my shoulders after too much brushing. One of the women, tall and pale with a round moon face, broke the sharp awkward silence and told me to follow her. When I hesitated, she beckoned with her finger. We walked down another hallway to a bathroom where she positioned me in front of a long rectangular mirror mounted over several sinks.

"You are very lucky," she said, placing her hands on my shoulders while she stood behind me. "Not all children get to come to Synanon." A tight feeling squeezed my insides, but I managed to nod. Seeming satisfied, the woman opened a drawer and pulled out a large pair of scissors. A sense that something very bad was about to happen pricked my skin. I wondered how much longer it would be until my mother came back.

"Would you like to be a Synanon kid?" Her eyes narrowed, her gaze sweeping over my body.

Barely nodding, I fixed my gaze on her fingers looped through the scissors' handles.

"I'm so glad," she said, picking up a lock of my hair.

The cold flat metal of the scissors rested against my scalp as she cut into my dark thick curls and a chunk of hair fluttered down to the bathroom counter. She snipped quickly, hair spilling onto my shoulders and hands and around my feet.

"I am going to make you beautiful," she said under her breath. "Bald girls are beautiful."

Unable to find my voice, I simply stared at the blunt tufts of hair sticking out from my head. She procured an electric clipper and turned it on. It buzzed and vibrated as she slid it easily over my scalp, leaving a path of smooth brown skin. In minutes, I was bald.

In the mirror, a different little girl stared back at me, a girl whose head was too small for the rest of her body, her dark eyes now seemingly enlarged. I had become an alien like the others. I didn't want to look at my reflection, but I couldn't stop staring.

The woman bent down to my level. Her eyes glowed with an intensity I would later learn to recognize as fanaticism.

"Look how beautiful you are now."

I knew she was lying, trying to make me feel better about what she had done. Why had she done it, I wanted to ask, but I couldn't seem to talk. I wanted to tell her I needed to go home—that I'd changed my mind; I didn't want to be at Synanon anymore. Where was my mom? My thoughts clamored like frantic spectators at a show where things had gone drastically wrong. My words were stuck.

"Today you are a new person, a Synanon kid. Today is your birthday," the woman said. It wasn't my birthday. My birthday was in October.

"It's your Synanon birthday," she explained, as if she could read my thoughts. "Now what do you say?"

I had no idea what she meant or what she wanted me to tell her. I felt numb.

"You're welcome," she said in the absence of the "thank you" she'd anticipated from me. She smiled and watched for my reaction.

I stretched my lips, imitating the woman, and the haunted-eyed alien in the mirror smiled back. I didn't want to be her, so I looked away.

After brushing me off and cleaning up the mess of my shorn hair, she took my hand again and led me back to the other children, who hovered around me. One spoke up, asking, "Who's going to be her buddy?"

"Theresa will decide," the woman said.

My mother returned shortly, much to my relief. In her arms she carried a box that held everything necessary for making popcorn. I immediately ran to her side. She oohed and aahed over my new appearance, although I felt embarrassed to my very core.

"We are going to have a party to celebrate your coming to stay with us and your new birthday," she said, seeming not to notice my discomfort. "But first I want to introduce you to a special friend of mine. This is Sophie. She's going to be your buddy."

I looked at the chubby, potbellied child with the large, round head and round, rosy cheeks. So it's a girl, I thought. She had been clinging to my mom ever since she'd come back into the room, and watching her, a faint feeling of jealousy tickled at my throat. I wanted to be the one at my mother's side. I was her daughter, not this boyish-looking girl who possessively held her arm. As Sophie's round, eager eyes took me in she leaned in closer to my mother, claiming the space.

My silence hardly mattered because Sophie talked non-stop; there was little chance for me to get a word out, even if I'd wanted to. My mother busied herself setting up refreshments and Sophie grabbed my hand, her smile revealing severely bucked teeth, which I later learned were due to her habitual thumb sucking. She yanked me to her side and asked, "Do you want to help make the popcorn?" Her dark eyes jumped about with an agitated excitement that reminded me of my cousin Joey's hamster.

I picked up the bag of popcorn only to have Sophie snatch it out of my hands. "Do you want to pour the popcorn?" She looked up at my mother.

"Celena, why don't you get the oil," my mom said.

"I'll get it." Sophie angled me out of the way, grabbing the bottle. I wandered off.

Sophie returned to my side, linking her arm with mine. "I am going to be your best friend," she informed me, patting my hand as if to prove her point. With unusual strength, she pulled me back to the popcorn setup. Every time I attempted to talk with my mom, Sophie interrupted. If I said or examined anything, Sophie was right there with me, imitating my movements, copying my mannerisms, repeating everything, constantly interrupting and giggling. After an hour I began to despise her, the gummy bucked smile and anxious chubby hands grabbing at me. I pulled my arm from her with such force that she stumbled back. "Leave me alone!"

I felt as if I were a doll for Sophie to do with as she pleased. I wanted to go home. The perpetual smile vanished from Sophie's face. My mother's face seemed to collapse with disappointment.

"I don't want her to be my buddy. Make her leave me alone." My throat closed with the tears I fought to keep back.

Sophie's shoulders sagged, her eyes darting from me to my mom and the other children, who hung back, non-interactive and uninterested now that I was as bald as they were.

"Oh, but Sophie's such a good friend," my mother said, squatting to our level and taking both our hands. "She's all prepared to show you around and explain how everything works, and she's been looking forward to your arrival. The two of you will be sharing a room, and soon you'll enjoy each other's company."

I didn't want to share a room with Sophie, and I didn't want to be a beautiful Synanon girl. I stared at Sophie, doubtful. It seemed she wanted to be me. I had not considered it possible to be given a good friend. I decided that I hated her.

THE NEXT DAY I found myself again in the large room where the odd party had taken place the previous evening. I sat on a metal folding chair as part of a circle that contained my mother, two other adults and some children.

"We are going to play a game," said the woman who had shaved my head.

"We don't use the titles "mom" and "dad" or "mister" and "missus" here. We use our first names only. I'm Linda, and this is Theresa." She waved toward my mother, who sat waiting expectantly. "Understand?"

I did not understand, so I said nothing.

"This is a special game. Here, you can say anything. Any words you like. You can say *shit* and *fuck* if you want. Try it. Say those words."

Linda waited.

I waited.

"Try it," she urged, as if she were asking me to recite a nursery rhyme.

I shook my head.

"You must be very angry with your mother for leaving you for such a long time."

I folded my hands tightly in my lap, squeezing my fingers as if I could wring out my confusion and frustration.

"We all know that you are angry." Linda's brows drew together, creating a deep crease in her forehead. "We don't keep anger bottled up here."

I decided it was best to stay quiet. I didn't know what she was talking about.

"All right, I'll have a turn," Linda said. She turned to my mother. "Theresa, look at what you've done to your daughter. Do you know how much you've fucked her up?"

My mother flinched as if someone had flicked water in her face. Then she recovered, her mouth quivering back into a smile.

I bit my lip, tasting blood. Little girls didn't say words like that. When I'd heard cuss words in the past, my first reaction had been to throw my hands over my mouth. I couldn't remember a time when I didn't know that cuss words were nasty. This woman, Linda, demanded that I say things that back home would have earned me a mouth washing with soap.

When I remained silent, one of the other children said, "Last night there wasn't enough fucking popcorn. I hardly got any."

This remark set off a litany of complaints from the other kids, who then turned on each other, remembering old slights and recalling incidents that brought them to a pitch of boiling fury.

"You poop-head!" one of them screamed.

"I know you are, but what am I!"

"You stole my money!"

"I told you, for the last time, I never took your stinking money, you stupid asshole!"

The children began to scream, fighting to be heard. A few of them rocked manically in their chairs. One boy balled his hand into a fist and hit it against his palm while he yelled. Another snarled, baring tiny milk teeth.

The high-pitched sound of someone yelling "Shit, shit, shit, shit" caught my attention. Across from me, the chanter's eyes widened, boring into mine, the bald head tilting crazily from side to side. I didn't know whether it was a boy or girl. "Shit, shit, shit."

I shrank back in my chair.

Linda leaned forward. "Quiet!" The screaming continued. "I said quiet!" The arguing and yelling tapered off.

Turning to me, Linda motioned with an open hand toward my mother. "What would you like to say to Theresa, Celena? Do you want to let her know how you feel about her leaving you for so long? You can say anything you want. Tell her, 'Fuck you.' Speak freely."

I shook my head, grimacing, and closed my eyes, trying to make it all disappear. But it didn't. Instead, the other children started yelling at one another again. After a while most of them had exhausted themselves into a temporary quiet as a few talked about their irritations. Some listened attentively, offering advice or stating their disagreements more reasonably. Even when they were just talking, their words were blunt and crude.

From time to time, Linda said, "Good," or "Okay." Then she announced the game was over.

I stood with the others, my legs rubbery from the aftereffects of adrenaline, which surged through my muscles. The children hugged and kissed one another or shook hands. "Good game!" they repeated, over and over. It was not clear to me what game we had been playing, why the game had ended or who had won.

My mother hugged me and told me in her soft voice that I had done well. Once she'd released me from her embrace, others came to congratulate me.

"Don't worry. You'll get better," one of the children said and shook my hand.

The sound of singing cut through the congratulatory conversation. A woman carrying a small round fruitcake had entered the room. Her face was illuminated with smiles. "It's your Synanon birthday. We're so glad you're here," she said.

The others joined in. "It's your Synanon birthday. You've been here one day. It's your Synanon birthday. You came here on a door. Celena! Celena! We wish you many more!" The song ended with clapping, whistling and laughter.

I stood among the grinning bald people, hoping to go home. I wanted my dad. I wanted to walk outside and see large buildings, neighborhoods and streets with cars, not the view of the unfamiliar empty landscape outside the sliding glass doors.

I had never encountered people like these Synanon people, not on the streets in Compton or Inglewood, not on TV and not in a storybook. While slices of cake were passed around, I tried to make sense of the scramble of odd occurrences that had taken place, realization seeping in. Bald and clad in overalls like everyone else, I held my paper plate, celebrating a birthday that didn't exist, finally absorbing the fact that I was staying.

CHAPTER TWO

The Demonstrator

"I AM A DEMONSTRATOR," Linda said. "My job is to demonstrate to you how to be a good Synanon member. There is a lot to learn, but your buddy will help you."

Sophie stood by, fidgeting while Linda gave me this speech. We were in the room Sophie and I shared, where I'd spent the last two nights lying beneath a thin gray blanket on a hard narrow bed, with Sophie chattering incessantly. For the last few days I had scarcely been able to do anything without her shadowing me.

"Will I see my mom?" I asked.

"You mean Theresa?" Linda waited for me to say my mother's name, but I stood before her, silent and sad. She squatted so we were at eye level. "Here in Synanon, all adults are your parents. You don't need a mom and dad. Whenever you want something, you can come and get me or another demonstrator."

I was beyond bewildered and couldn't seem to make sense of

anything. Before I'd been brought to Synanon, my father had driven me to my Uncle Danny's home in Riverside to spend the weekend. We'd arrived in the afternoon, and my father and uncle had spent an hour or so talking and drinking coffee while I'd played with my cousins. Before my father left, he hugged and kissed me and shook my uncle's hand, thanking him and my aunt for their hospitality. Later that night my mom and Mary Ann had stopped by and taken me with them when they left. I'd thought she had told me we were to visit Synanon. Had she said we would live here?

After the party celebrating my Synanon birthday, my mother had vanished. I couldn't remember her saying goodbye or telling me when she might come back. I went over the events again and again like a connect-the-dots picture, searching for something I'd missed. How long would I be in Synanon and why hadn't my father called to see how I was?

The second night I inevitably began to cry as the enormity of the situation weighed on me, and try as I might to contain my sobs in my pillow, Sophie eventually woke up and tiptoed across the floor. Her weight sank into the mattress as she sat down and leaned over to stroke my brow.

"What's wrong?" she asked.

"I want to see my mom."

"Don't worry. Theresa will come back."

Sophie's words did not console me.

My limited possessions that I'd brought to Synanon, not only my clothes, but also my most treasured baby doll, had been confiscated. In place of my own things, I'd received a stack of clothing that matched that of the other children.

Linda pulled out one of the drawers in Sophie's dresser. All of her white t-shirts were rolled tightly into tubular forms and stacked neatly end-to-end.

"This is how we keep our clothes," Linda said. "Sophie will show you how to roll them."

Linda pulled out another drawer, which held all of Sophie's pants, rolled the same way. Before she closed the drawers, Linda glanced at me. Then she said, "Sophie, I would like you to show Celena how to roll her clothes. I'll be back later to see how she's getting along."

Sophie, ever smiling, opened my dresser and grabbed a stack of the drab gray overalls and blue jeans, clothing very different from the short, colorful, knee-length dresses I was accustomed to wearing. I found that I'd subconsciously developed the habit of raising my hand to the smooth surface of my scalp, sliding over the whole of it as if to receive further confirmation that all my hair actually had been shaved off.

I looked down at the baggy overalls I wore. They reminded me of the nursery song "Old McDonald Had a Farm." I watched my roommate's puffy small hands as she expertly folded, rolled and tucked a shirt into its own self-contained tube. Laughing, she tossed it and it fell to my bed, bouncing off the blanket that was pulled tight and wrinkle-free with the corners folded over like pockets.

"They're called 'hospital corners,'" Sophie told me.

I practiced rolling the clothes until I had a shirt as smooth and cylindrical as those produced by my ever-ebullient buddy.

As promised, Linda returned to examine my work. She picked up a rolled shirt and ran her finger under the fold. It held. She set it down, her gaze flicking over the rest of the tubular clothing. "Very good."

That I'd pleased her gave me courage. "When will I see Theresa?" I hoped that using my mother's name would produce the desired effect of getting some information from Linda. Instead, the pleased smile left her lips, her mouth tightened with disapproval.

"The sooner you are used to being apart from Theresa, the better. I told you, mothers do not matter here. We are all your mothers. Isn't that better than just having one?"

I did not want a group of mothers I didn't know. My mother, Theresa, loved me. It showed in her eyes and body language. But after our reunion, she was gone again, replaced like a pair of shoes. I did not know what to say to Linda, who coldly demanded that she, in a sense, was now my new mom. A feeling of terror came over me. I clenched my fingers into my palms to fight back the tears that filled my eyes.

"When we have another game, you can talk about it," Linda said. "That's when you get out your feelings."

I took a deep breath, not daring to move.

"Tell Sophie 'Thank you,'" Linda said.

I couldn't speak. Afraid that instead of words there would be just an uncontrollable wail, I held myself very still.

Linda gave me a minute. "It is important when someone shows you how to do something properly that you thank them."

"Thank you," I whispered.

CHAPTER THREE

Inspection and the Schedule

I AWOKE TO A LOUD CLANGING. Though it was still dark outside, a light from the hall illuminated my room in a soft glow. For a moment, I wasn't sure where I was.

Linda stood in the doorway holding a large cowbell and hitting it with a metal rod, her movements measured and methodical. Sophie was already out of bed. As Linda left our doorway, clanging as she moved to the next room, I watched my roommate pad over to me, a silhouetted figure in shadowy lighting.

"It's time to get up," she said. "We have to get ready for inspection."

I removed my bed covers and glimpsed several girls still in their gowns running down the hallway.

Sophie turned on the overhead light and I watched as she briskly made her bed. Without turning, she told me to make up my own bed. She looked over my work, pulled a little at the gray blanket to unfurl a wrinkle and tucked in the corners tighter, emphasizing the crispness of the folds. This constant quest for perfection puzzled me.

I followed her to the bathroom, where the three sinks were already in use, each with one or two girls vigorously brushing their teeth. The other children eyed me, but their curiosity was gone.

We shrugged off our gowns, and I stepped in line behind the other naked girls waiting to enter the massive shower room. Each stood naturally, some yawning. They were used to this strange situation.

I didn't know how to act or where to put my hands as I still hadn't grown used to the naked lineup. At my home, people didn't stand naked in a crowd. Everyone had privacy in the bathroom. The door always remained locked.

I needed to go number one and make a BM. I peered over my shoulder at the room where the toilets were. I already knew what was there: two toilets with no doors. I wasn't sure I could go to the bathroom with other people watching me.

Several girls emerged from the showers, their bodies slick and dripping wet. Our group was next. There were five showerheads and thick bars of green soap in holders. In an instant, the enormous stall fogged with steam. I wrapped one of the short, thin white towels around my body and tiptoed to the toilets. A girl sat on one of them, wiping herself. I turned to leave.

"Look," she called out. I glanced over my shoulder. Her cheeks indented in a dimpled smile, she held the paper smeared brown with feces. "It's poop," she chirped. Unsure what to say, I turned around and scurried to my room, where I finished getting ready for the inspection. Sophie had already dressed. Wielding a white rag, she dusted our dressers, nightstands and lamps, glimpsing now and then at the cloth. "The demonstrator always checks to make sure that everything is clean and that our clothes have no dirt or stains." I looked down at my overalls and didn't see any spots or dirt marks. My tennis shoes were creased and a bit scuffed. They were obviously a second-hand pair.

Sophie handed me some shoe polish. "Do you know how to polish your shoes?" When I shook my head, she uncapped the little bottle and showed me how to dab at the shoe with the attached sponge and work the polish into the creases with a rag. When she'd finished, she recapped the polish and put it away.

"Time for inspection!" someone called out.

Girls ran up and down the hallway, darting into their bedrooms. Sophie shoved me in the direction of my bed and stood in front of hers. Her small, chubby body went rigid as she held her arms ramrod straight at her sides and stretched her neck as if to appear taller while staring straight ahead at nothing. I took the same stance and heard girls moving about the neighboring rooms before a hush descended upon the dorm.

Some minutes later, Demonstrator Linda entered our room. She was all business as her gaze fell on me. "Stand up straight."

I pulled my frame a little straighter, trying to stretch my neck as I'd seen Sophie do.

"Open your mouth," Linda said.

I did, keeping my gaze fixed straight ahead. Linda's face came close to mine while she squatted to peer for what felt like a long time at the inside of my mouth.

"Smile," she said.

"What?" I whispered.

Linda stood up. "Sophie, come over here."

Sophie walked over to us and stood facing me.

"Show Celena."

Sophie's cheeks bunched up into the obligatory smile.

Linda nodded and told me to do the same.

I grimaced while she squatted to examine my teeth. "Good. Turn around."

I did.

"Good."

She looked at my bed. "Nice and tight. Good job, Sophie, for helping your buddy."

Sophie beamed.

"You are excused. You may go to breakfast now," Linda said.

"Come on," Sophie said, making a grab for my hand. I pulled it away, but followed her outside into the cold winter morning. Other children emerged from the buildings cloistered next to ours. All of us wore overalls and white t-shirts as well as an overshirt or jacket. Due to the uniformity of our clothing and haircuts, I still wasn't sure which children were girls and which were boys. Sophie and I joined the merging group on the road and walked a quarter-mile to the Commons, the building where we had our meals.

Only children, supervised by demonstrators, ate in the Commons. The tables were long and U-shaped, each with little pushed-in plastic chairs. We were allowed to sit wherever we wanted.

A woman circulated through the room, handing out colorful, hard-plastic cups of milk.

"No, thank you," I told her.

"There is no breakfast until you drink your milk," she said.

I swallowed and took the cup. I hated milk. Some of the children were already chugging theirs. As each finished, he or she was rewarded with a plate of scrambled eggs and piece of toast. I took a sip; it tasted sweet and watery, even worse than the milk I'd had in the past. I set the cup down, feeling nausea rise in waves.

"Plug your nose," someone said.

I looked up. It was Poop Girl.

"If you plug your nose and drink it, you can't taste it," she said.

She pinched her nostrils and downed the milk. When she finished, her upper lip was swathed in dewy white.

I followed suit. Several gulps in, the cold sticky sweetness felt like a wad of mucus. I didn't want to gag because I was afraid the milk might come back up my throat.

"I'll drink it," Sophie offered. Her eager, round-eyed gaze darted about the room. When the demonstrator's back was turned, she quickly finished my milk and slapped the empty cup down next to my hand.

Moments later we were both served plates of soupy scrambled eggs and half pieces of toast. Worse than a cup of milk is a cup of milk and eggs. I pushed them around and took a bite of toast, willing myself not to barf it up.

The meal seemed to last forever.

After breakfast we took another fairly long walk up a hill to the classrooms. My grade was in a room that seemed to favor the look of wooden desks and wooden chairs on a wood floor. Large picture windows without curtains displayed a gray morning sky.

For our math lesson, we counted out small wooden cubes into groups of ten. Later there was a physical education class, which consisted mostly of one exercise, step-ups, that we performed until my legs ached and became numb. Afterward, we took showers again. Then we played the game, screaming at each other until dinner, followed bedtime at 8 p.m.

Several days went by and my mother didn't return. The demonstrators constantly reminded not to call her "Mom." "Her name is Theresa," I was told. "And don't ask about her anymore."

CHAPTER FOUR

B^{efore}

WHEN I STRETCH my mind back to the fragmented images of my early years before Synanon, I see my mom in snapshots, reading to me while I sit on her lap, her finger tracing the words, her long brown hair trailing across the pages. The paper emits a sweet, faintly musky smell, an odor that encapsulates comfort for me. She's in the kitchen of our studio apartment, making cinnamon toast for breakfast and serving it on a napkin. My mother has something ephemeral, almost childlike, about her. A vein of vulnerability runs through her that even at age three I am able to intuit.

For the most part, we were alone, the two of us adrift in the sea of humanity that makes up Los Angeles, isolated in our urban poverty. We moved often, from Hollywood to Long Beach to downtown. Once, when we'd settled into an apartment complex, a woman came to our door. "This is a family place," she said. Her arms were folded, her hair straightened into a stiff, perfect, shiny helmet that framed her dark, self-righteous face. Her eyes told us that she was closer to God than we could ever be.

"We don't want you loose harlots and your bastard children here," she shouted. "You hear me? Your kind's not wanted here. You're nothing but a yellow nigger with green eyes and good hair. You're not foolin' anybody." The encounter left my mother looking frail, the smile with which she'd greeted the woman disappearing as she eased the door closed.

"Why did that lady yell at you, Mommy?"

The only answer I received was a hug.

Too young to know we struggled to live our lives, I had no idea my mother shielded me from certain realities. For me, she'd spin pleasant fantasies. We had no money to buy things that weren't necessities, but window-shopping turned our lack of funds into a game. We could pretend to purchase the things we saw on display. We went for picnics in the park, meeting placid, idle women in crocheted tops and homespun dresses, sunning themselves, with children as old as me still nursing in their mothers' arms. In the rain, blocks away from home, we listened to the drops fall on our umbrellas and splashed through or leaped over puddles. Games were my mother's way of keeping me from feeling the cold and tedium of long walks in unpleasant weather. If I grew tired, my mother lifted me to her hip and let me rest my head on her shoulder, her long dark hair draping my arms or whipping about in the wind, obscuring my vision of cars that whizzed past us. In a pinch, we hitchhiked.

My attachment was primordial, existential, a sensory umbilical cord of warmth, touch and scent that filled the minimal span between us. I luxuriated in the softness of her skin, the combined warmth of our body heat, and the moist and slightly sour scent of saliva when I sucked my two middle fingers while patting her breast.

Sometimes, I went to daycare; other times, not. Once, my mother told me she had quit one of her many temporary jobs because she couldn't bear to wake me in the mornings before she left for work, which often set me to crying. She wanted to be sure that we were friends, that she lived with me in my child's world where everything appeared new, exciting and ripe for exploration.

Possibly she sought to reclaim a childhood she had not lived properly herself. At fourteen years old, my mother was forced into the maternal role of caring for her brothers after my grandmother Gladys was struck down in her prime by debilitating depression, taking to her bed for years. The smothering sadness returned to stalk Theresa during her own experience of motherhood.

I have vague recollections of the various men in whose homes we stayed. A house on stilts, the door in the kitchen opening to a spindly forest of trees, with no balcony to block a bone-breaking fall. A bowl of sprouts left on the table for me to eat, my mother and her friend behind his closed bedroom door.

Alone in the hum of silence, I watched faint dust funnels swirl in the fading light. When the door opened and her friend emerged, his long, dusky brown hair spilling over pale naked shoulders, I ran to the futon bed where my mother lay curled under blankets. She lifted them for me and I wiggled myself into the curve of her body. Later we sat cross-legged on the bed, accepting her friend's offerings of little white boxes, neat and compact like birthday presents, with the flaps open, long thin sticks thrusting out of them. Inside one of the boxes was something slick and gelatinous. The other held rice mixed with bits of carrots and pink, crescent-shaped things. I poked my finger into the slimy stuff.

"Chinese food," he said, also sitting cross-legged, his penis, shrunken and limp, tucked away under a thick cloud of pubic hair.

At the house of a different friend, my mother washed dishes, completely at home in his kitchen. I wandered into the yard: a jumble of unattended shrubbery, dead grass and dirt patches. On the inside crease of my left arm is a pale little wrinkle, a scar where his dog bit me. I remember nothing of the attack, only the man shaking me so hard afterward that I was too shocked to cry.

"What did I tell you, huh? Huh?" he demanded. "You were teasing him. That's why he bit you. I told you not to tease my dog."

Beyond him my mother watched, her eyes mirroring my fear. When she stepped forward to reach for me, he yanked me out of her grasp. "I'll take care of it."

She said nothing, the color gone from her face. Instead she stood very still while he whisked me down the hallway to the bathroom and poked his finger into the jagged bits of my torn flesh, blood spooling up from the wound. I held myself rigid as he lifted me up to thrust my arm under the faucet, turning on the water and washing the bite with a white sludge of melted soap.

"Little brat," he hissed, and he dried the wound, slapping on a bandage before prodding me toward his bedroom, where he sat me on the bed, rough as a sack of rocks. "You stay here until it's time for you to go."

I shuddered and tried not to breathe as I watched him walk away and close the door. Long minutes ticked by. I didn't dare move.

When the door creaked open, I held my breath and focused on the carpet, but the person who entered was my mother, smiling, with an apology tucked into the corners of her lips.

"Hi," she whispered.

I remained silent; the thought of her friend rushing in to yell at us kept me mute.

"He didn't mean it." She slipped into the room, closing the door with a quiet click and sat next to me. "Do you want some gum?"

She dug into her jeans pocket for a pack of Juicy Fruit and pulled a slim silver stick from the cheerful yellow jacket, ripping it in half and handed me my portion.

I took it wordlessly, unwrapped it and popped the powdery pale bit of treat into my mouth.

"It's okay," she said a little louder. "Just wait here like he said. We're going to leave soon." Satisfied that I was placated, she smiled, putting a finger to her lips, and she left as quietly as she came in.

Between apartments we sometimes stayed with my grandmother Gladys, crowding onto her sofa bed. I would not come to recognize my grandmother's fun side, her love of jazz and preference for Miles Davis over Bing Crosby during the Christmas holidays, until I was much older. She took a girlish pleasure in dancing, putting on family skits and, believing her feet to be her best feature, decorating her toes with rings.

As a small child, I knew her only as dour Gladys, with her tight headscarves, drab clothes and large purses that hung flat and old-ladyish from her shoulder. I spent long days in her apartment, an interior of beige blandness. The plastic artificial flowers placed on the coffee table and end table to brighten the place had only added to the feeling of lifelessness. I recall sitting for hours with a small bag of candy to keep me quiet while she rocked away the hours in her rocking chair, frowning to herself. My grandmother hated cooking, so we ate most of our meals at Thrifty's Drug Store.

Catching sight of my mother wearing blue jeans could set my grandmother off on a tirade accompanied by tears. "Where did I go wrong?" she wailed. "God have mercy! You're a good Catholic girl, Theresa; that's how I raised you. You got to stick with your own kind—Creole people." My mother would roll her eyes and I'd laugh. Her distress was so overstated that it held a comical quality.

"The devil has the chile, Theresa. She's an imp," my grandmother yelled when I giggled over her ravings.

"She's a child, Mama," my mother said. I'd dance around my grandmother, making faces, teasing her, hoping she'd lose her temper, while my mother lounged on the sofa.

"You see?" my grandmother said. "You see what she's doing? You better teach that little imp a lesson: slap her behind."

When she made a grab for me, I darted away, too quickly for her to catch. She'd stumble forward, clutching nothing but air, then give up and break into melodramatic sobs.

Her despair fascinated me. Normal, everyday things like my braided kinky hair, fitted at the ends with colorful plastic barrettes, made her nervous. At night, I awoke to her unwinding my small braids while praying to the saints for salvation before settling down to sleep.

Often she stood hunched over the bathroom sink, washing her hands repeatedly while muttering Hail Marys. Other times she fingered the glass beads, creaking to and fro in her rocking chair and frowning at the injustices of her life.

The Catholic churches I attended with my grandmother matched her melancholy mood with their poorly lit, cavernous interiors, stained glass windows and portraits of sad-looking saints. Behind the altar, Jesus hung on the cross, imbued with eternal sorrow.

Expected to sit still on a hard bench for the hour we spent at church services, I inevitably swung my legs and received sharp pinches from my grandmother's quick fingers. As we rose, knelt, rose, sat and sang with the other congregants, our voices reached to the high ceiling and outward, the echoes circulating like mournful ghosts. If I fidgeted again, my grandmother's hand closed firmly around my wrist, cutting off circulation.

I preferred my mother's version of God as a friend who lived around the corner. When I recited the traditional prayer "Now I lay me down to sleep, I pray the Lord my soul to keep. If I should die before I wake, I pray the Lord my soul to take," my mother stopped me. She didn't want me to be on my knees contemplating my possible death. "God is your friend, Celena," she said. "When you pray, you're having a conversation with God. Prayer is like making a phone call."

She created a small book of green construction paper with the pages hole-punched and tied together with yarn. Glued to them were photographs of me engaged in various activities: smelling a flower, petting a llama at the zoo, laughing hysterically. Under each, she wrote a brief caption: "God loves flowers." "God loves animals." "God has a sense of humor." My mother's motto: "If you want to know God, get to know yourself."

My father inhabited the world of relatives; he held the status of a scarcely seen favorite uncle. When he visited, his personality seemed almost too big for our little studio apartment. He laughed loud and talked loud, his cologne and aftershave clotting the air around him, tickling my nasal passages. On his knee my father would place me for a pretend horse ride, or up into the air he'd throw me, making wide eyes at me as I came crashing back into his arms.

Most of our visits took place in his apartment, neatly furnished with white brocade sofas and matching throw pillows carefully arranged. Plastic runners protected stretches of frequently vacuumed carpet. He didn't understand my mother's way of keeping house: clothes strewn about, dishes piled in the sink, books stacked on the toilet seat lid; nor could he understand the fact that my mother never really had a plan.

We drifted, my mother and I. On one occasion, I recall my

father squatting next to our car, peering into the window at my mother seated behind the steering wheel. "Where are you going?" he asked.

"Not sure," my mother said.

He looked at me, his grin a question mark. "Those earrings are too big on Celena."

My dress was too big as well; the top slipped off my shoulders, the costume jewelry brushed against my bare skin. My mother started the car. Without a goodbye, we glided coolly away. I craned my neck, watching him recede into the background as he remained on the sidewalk, hands in his pockets. When he noticed me staring at him, his face lit up and he waved.

I waved back.

On one of my irregular afternoon visits to my father's home, I discarded my clothes and breezed through the living room, looking for something to do. He'd been lounging on his sofa, watching soaps, but shot up when I went by.

"Where are your clothes?" he asked.

I shrugged, unable to decipher the alarm in his voice.

"Oh, no." He walked over to me, his mouth turned down hard, and took my arm, leading me back to the bedroom. "You can't walk around naked. Understand?" My clothes lay in a puddle of fabric on the carpet. "Put these things back on."

"But it's hot," I said.

"Little girls need to be dressed. Does your mother let you run around like this?"

I wiggled back into my clothes. I'd never given any thought to nudity, but at my father's it was wrong.

My mind struggled to reconcile the dichotomy of my parents' separate lives, as I was too young to comprehend that there would never be a connection. My mother diverged from the straight and narrow long before I had been born. The young woman my father met at a nightclub seven years earlier no longer existed. Soon I'd be living with him, but none of us knew that then.

ANXIETY SWALLOWED my mother bit by bit. A prescription for antidepressants—too strong—only enhanced her despair. A side effect caused her muscles to freeze up and her mouth to remain locked open like a rusted gate that could no longer shut, her eyes staring, life diminished to a flat gaze. I learned to busy myself or sit and wait until the spell broke.

At a trip to Denny's, my mother sat looking at the menu one moment, the next she'd turned into a statue.

The waitress approached our table and stared at the frozen woman across from me. "Ma'am, can you speak?"

Mouth agape, a silent scream, lips as taut as those of a corpse. That was my mother.

"Ma'am?"

I didn't know how to explain that she would eventually come back to life. I could only sit and hope the waitress would somehow figure it out.

When the paramedics arrived and guided my mother's Tin Man–like figure to the ambulance, a hush fell over the restaurant. A fierce protectiveness rose in my chest. I wanted to stomp away all the silent diners' eyes. "Stop looking at us!" I screamed.

When my mother finally decided to go to Synanon—"the people business," as the commune liked to refer to itself—she told me plainly that she had to leave me with my father and wasn't sure when we would see each other again. By the time the taxi arrived at my father's apartment in Inglewood, I'd worked myself into a fevered pitch of agitation, begging her not to go.

My father demanded I stop all that nonsense while my mother hugged me one last time, a pained expression on her face, and walked out of his apartment.

I ran after her, twisting the door knob, which held firm. Panicked, I let loose a piercing shriek, quieting only when my father threatened me with a whipping.

Synanon made my mother choose: either leave me and take advantage of the help they offered, or battle her crippling depression on her own.

CHAPTER FIVE

My Father's Story

MY FATE as a Synanon kid was etched into the blueprint of my life long before I existed. Over the years, through my mother and father's narrative of their inauspicious beginnings with the cult, I was able to piece together my peculiar destiny.

During visits with my father in my young teen years, a favorite activity of ours was to look at his family photo album. He would also produce a folder that contained pictures of the women he'd dated. Each photo he presented for my viewing came with a short story, piecing together his life though his long-ago love interests. Inevitably, he'd get to a picture of my mother, a black-and-white snapshot of her in a bikini on the beach, her dark hair pulled back in a ponytail and a demure expression on her face.

"Your mother was the most beautiful woman I'd ever seen," he'd say. "My friends used to ask me, 'Man, where'd you find her?' She turned heads everywhere she went. And she really loved me, but...." He'd crinkle his brow and shake his head, his habitual response whenever the subject of my mother came up.

"There was something," he went on. "I couldn't put my finger on it. She just wasn't the right girl for me. For one, she was too quiet. But she was beautiful, there's no doubt about that, and you inherited her looks, Celena. You have some of her mannerisms too. The way you sit, tilt your head to the side with your index finger at your temple, that's your mother all over."

My parents met at a club called Maverick's Flat on Crenshaw. They both loved nightlife and went out dancing every weekend, if not at a club, then at a house party. In the 1960s, South Central pulsed with music; young people packed the clubs, showing off their moves to the cha-cha, mashed potato, the twist and loco-motion.

Theresa was twenty years old, with a slim, petite figure, fine features, greenish eyes and dark shoulder-length hair, a Natalie Wood look-alike.

When my father, Jim, first glimpsed her, he told me he thought he'd witnessed an angel. He spent the next hour at the club searching for the elusive beauty. When a friend talked him into meeting a particular girl later that evening, he reluctantly agreed. The girl turned out to be Theresa. My father's handsome looks, big beaming smile and brown eyes, glistening with warmth and playfulness, must have cut instantly through my mother's natural shyness.

Their romance remained a secret for their first year together. Although they both came from a Creole background in Louisiana, my father's darker skin disqualified him as a suitor in my maternal grandfather's opinion. He didn't want his daughter to date anyone outside of their community of light-skinned Creoles. When the two men were first introduced, my grandfather refused to shake my father's hand, and in a fit of dramatic fury threatened to kill my mother if she continued to date him. They went on seeing each other despite my grandfather's violent reaction.

As an older child, I heard my grandfather say repeatedly, "The blacks are nothing but trouble, and the whites are not much better." And my grandmother liked to often remind me of my Creole status: "You have dark skin, but you're still Creole. It says on your birth certificate: Mother, Creole; Father, Negro."

Their deep obsession with ethnicity and internalized racism mystified me as a girl. In Synanon, race was not an issue. I realized my grandparents' ethnocentric focus was a reaction to a foregone time of strict societal segregation and the danger of passing for white in the Jim Crow South. In the 1930s, a black man's life in Louisiana was worth little. A duck hunter in his youth, my grandfather on occasion found the body of a black man suspended from a cypress tree or floating on the still waters, murdered and left to rot in the hushed swelter of the swamps.

According to my father, Theresa's beauty and fairer skin immediately pleased his mother, and over time my grandfather warmed to my father, as most did, for he had a sunny, charismatic disposition.

My parents dated for three years. During that time, new ideas that Theresa wanted to explore—Eastern spirituality, meditation, awareness groups and psychology—swept through American society. When she tried to talk to my father about her interests, the topics seemed too foreign for him to grasp. He couldn't relate to the "strange" concepts she brought up, notions like "money has no real value" and "Catholicism is dying and people don't need it to experience spirituality." To a deeply Catholic man who aspired to have millions of dollars one day, this was "crazy talk." As Theresa gradually lost interest in the American status quo, my father continued to embrace mainstream values.

By the winter of 1969, their relationship ended, and although they were no longer a couple, they maintained an easy friendship.

"After your mother and I broke up," my father told me, "I tried to keep some distance, but she kept calling me, complaining of feeling lonely. So one day, I said, 'Look, I know of a club in Santa Monica. It's part of this organization called Synanon. I go there sometimes. They supply food, drink, and live music—all at no cost. Why don't you go? Just get out and mingle.'"

My dad would talk to Theresa's picture, deep in his story.

"'The only thing about this place is that the Synanon people use it to try to recruit you into their lifestyle, and believe me, Theresa, you don't want to get involved with them.' So, I tell your mother, 'Feign interest, nod, take advantage of all the free stuff, then go home.' 'Oh, no,' she tells me. 'I'm not going to bother with them. I'll just go check out the club.'"

Raising his eyebrows, my dad would set the picture on his glass coffee table and point at me as I sat listening to him on the white brocade sofa in his modish living room, large abstract paintings displayed stylishly on the textured white walls.

"Well, what happens? The next thing I know, your mother tells me she's joined their little club, and I said, 'Theresa, didn't I tell you not to get involved with those people? A bunch of wackos is what they are, running around in overalls, looking like Farmer John. Take over America, my foot. Do you think Americans are going to let a bunch of Howdy Doodys way off in left field take over our country?'"

At this point he'd go lecture mode. The commune had robbed him of his most precious asset, his daughter, and now that he had me back, he wanted to wrest every bit of Synanon doctrine from my mind. His lectures about the folly of the cult were forceful and persistent, a desperate scouring of my psyche.

"Do you know how many wars we fought with the English, the Spanish, the Indians to make and keep this country? A lot of people died, and the people at Synanon thought we were going to hand our country over to them. I like America just fine. It'll be over my dead body before I'd let a bunch of Loony Toons take over. And—" He'd jab the air with his finger. "—I'm not the only one who feels that way."

My father's monologue required no response from me. My job during these outbursts was only to sit and listen.

CHAPTER SIX

My Mother's Story
September, 2013; Phone Interview

WHEN I LEFT you with your father to move to Synanon, I was transferred to the Oakland facility. After I arrived, a woman searched through all my personal belongings and confiscated my prescription pills. She took me into the bathroom, where she wanted me to watch while she opened each bottle, emptied all my medications into the toilet and flushed the pills away.

Those pills were prescribed to me, and I should have been weaned off them gradually. Going cold turkey put me into a sort of catatonic state for months. Everything felt foggy, and I couldn't think clearly. I had a hard time following conversations, and life became like a strange dream.

I spent most of my days scrubbing cooking pots and dirty dishes. In the evenings, there were games, but they were different from the games at the club. There was a lot of screaming, swearing and verbal attacks, and I was kind of mute through it all.

People would attack me and I'd try to organize my thoughts, but I couldn't seem to form coherent speech.

I remember some guy calling another guy an asshole. That was the first time I'd heard that word, and the visual I got was stunning.

Then, one day, the fog in my mind lifted and everything became clear and ordered again. I joined a conversation between two other people I happened to be sitting with, and they were both surprised. Everyone was used to me having little or nothing to say.

Not too long after that, I started dating this young guy, Tom. He was maybe seventeen, I guess. I don't remember how the relationship started, but I got a lot of flak for going with someone so young.

Tom started talking up one of the other Synanon properties in Marin, the Tomales Bay property, where they had something called "boot camp." He raved about how much fun boot camp was, what a great time he'd had there and that I should apply.

After listening to him for a while, I thought maybe it would be nice to be outside in nature, working in the fresh air, so I applied.

My application was accepted, but the "boot camp" wasn't anything like what Tom had described. It wasn't fun at all. "Boot camp" was more like labor camp. It was a lot of heavy ranch work, military marching and compulsory long runs, and then in the evenings, when I was completely exhausted, we had to play the game.

I couldn't have my own private thoughts or feelings. The Synanon people were always trying to get me to admit to stuff that I shouldn't be thinking or feeling, and then they'd attack me for opening up. It was a constant teardown, and I started to really miss you, Celena.

I felt miserable that I was separated from you. It was almost unbearable at times. That was when I started to think about leaving, and when I started to think about that, it suddenly dawned on me that I didn't know how to leave. We lived on a ranch far from town, and if I wanted to leave the property, I had to have permission or be accompanied by a senior resident. I couldn't even make a private phone call.

What I mean is that we could leave, but it was a big deal to admit that you wanted to go. Usually, when people talked about wanting to quit the commune, there was a lot of persuasion to get them to stay, and they'd be subjected to more gaming. Community members would try to convince doubters that it was in their best interest to stay. Often people caved under that pressure, but there was another way: I could run away in the night.

Runaways were called "splittees," and a plan to split between two or more people was called a "contract," which was what I ended up making with another woman and a man. Our plan was to leave in the middle of the night and walk to the nearest town, Marshall, and from there catch a bus to San Francisco. But it never happened because the other woman started to feel guilty, and she broke our contract during a game.

After that, I was subjected to a series of teardown games and was told I wasn't good enough for boot camp. Management sent me back to Oakland. I still wanted to leave and probably would have if I hadn't met Barbara.

Barbara was an older woman with some status in the community, and she took a special interest in me. When I first met her, she said, "Honey, I've got my eye on you and I'm going to make it my mission to get you to stay here. You have too much potential for us to lose you."

It was the first time since I'd come to Synanon that I felt somebody cared about me. I told Barbara how much I missed you and how hard it was for me being separated from my child. Barbara told me that if I worked hard and truly embraced the

Synanon way that I would be reunited with you, and she promised to help me make that happen.

The more vested in the community I became, the more unattractive the outside world began to look. Sometimes when we had games or seminars in which the subject of mainstream living was brought up and we discussed how it destroys people, I'd remember how vulnerable and helpless I felt when I was on my own. Those thoughts hardened my resolve in doing the good work and to finally bring you into the community. It was in Oakland, where I met most of the people who would become my closest friends throughout my time in the community and after.

What really put a fire under me, though, was when I discovered the Kidsnatchers club, a kind of support group for parents working to bring their children into Synanon. The Kidsnatchers really gave me something to strive for, and I developed a Synanon zeal in the group. Once I became involved in Kidsnatchers, I started to get a lot of approval and encouragement from upper management. I finally began to feel on track with the movement.

Barbara breathed new life into me, and I became inspired all over again with Synanon, only this time instead of only going through the motions, I began to put in real effort to be the best Synanon citizen I could be.

CHAPTER SEVEN

Relatives

AT MY FATHER'S HOME, I had my own room, which I wasn't used to. Late at night, I'd creep into the bed he shared with his girlfriend, Alice, depositing my dolls and stuffed animals under their covers before shaking my father awake, complaining of ghosts and monsters and begging to sleep with them. Too tired to argue with me, he'd grumble an okay.

In the morning, I awoke to find my toys scattered everywhere and Alice scissoring the air with her legs, doing exercises.

Sometimes, she'd already left for work, so my father and I would be alone together. We developed a morning routine, a running joke between us, which consisted of checking each other's breath and pretending to fall over dead from the smell. I'd explode in giggles every time.

In the bathroom, my father lectured me on hygiene. After we scrubbed our teeth and gargled with minty mouthwash, he'd say,

"You want nice white teeth, Celena. When you grow up and start dating, no man is going to want to deal with yellow teeth."

I'd scrunch up my face while my dad watched me with mock seriousness before we both broke out laughing.

Settling my chin comfortably in my hand on the bathroom counter, I'd watch my father coat his face in white foam and glide his razor through the spicy-smelling shaving cream, leaving streaks of smooth brown skin. He'd wash off the residue, examine his mustache and comb his sideburns. If he put on a suit, we were going job hunting.

For breakfast, we ate the cornbread his mother, Regina, sent home with us after our Sunday dinners at my grandparents' house. We'd crumble the fluffy bread into bowls to be eaten like cereal with milk and sugar.

I spent long days riding around in my father's car while he looked for work and went to job interviews. Sometimes he'd leave me in the car with the window opened slightly, a bag of potato chips and soda to keep me company, along with a warning to stay put and not open the car door for anyone.

On weekends when Alice had free time, we went to her sister Stella's in Compton, and I played with the youngest of Stella's four children, Danielle, who was only two years older than me. Alice sometimes took Danielle and me to the beach or an amusement park. Other times we stayed home and hung out at the pool in the apartment complex.

Having never learned to swim, my father would sun himself on one of the white plastic pool chairs while Alice waded into the cool water, carrying me on her hip, my arms and legs wrapped like octopus tentacles around her body. Try as she might, she could not peel me off to begin my swimming lessons. I could see clear to the bottom of the pool and the dip of the cement alarmed me. I'd wiggle myself higher into Alice's arms to escape the water lapping against my shoulders.

My father laughed genially from the safety of his chair at my frantic attempts to cling to Alice. Sometimes he'd follow us along the perimeter, calling out encouragingly for me to kick my legs or place my face in the water. I could not trust him at these times. He wanted me to swim, but would not put even a toe into the water himself.

When we finally went inside, a warm towel would be wrapped around me, and with eyes burning from chlorine, I'd skitter to the bathroom, waiting for the comfort of the dry clothes Alice brought me. Soon all the terror of the swimming lesson was forgotten as I ate a hot baloney sandwich prepared by my father, the white bread soaked with grease and mayonnaise.

My life took on a regular rhythm as Alice eagerly stepped into the maternal role that my mother had vacated. She provided me with dolls whose blond hair I continually brushed until they were balding. My clothing, which Alice kept neatly folded in my dresser, smelled of Tide detergent and lavender. On weekends she plaited my hair into two braids and tied them with ribbons that matched the colors of my clothes. Among Alice's relatives, I was called her little girl. When I wanted comfort, I learned to go to Alice. Possibly, at such a young age, Alice and my mother blended into one and the same person for me. They looked very similar to each other, and I don't recall missing my mother with Alice around.

But one afternoon, just as suddenly as my mother had departed, Alice left too. My father and I returned to the apartment to find all the furniture gone. Alice had taken what belonged to her. In shock, I walked the length of our bare living room. Then I sat on the floor while my father paced, phone to ear, his jaw clenched with tension.

By the end of the week, my bags were packed. Jobless and struggling financially, he thought I might fare better under Alice's care, and so, like the furniture, I went too.

In Compton, where Alice's father, Lewis, had a house, I was given two rooms: a bedroom and a playroom equipped with every toy Alice thought I should possess, as well as a school desk and handwriting booklets. Alice valued education. Whenever I spoke, she corrected my grammar. "Black English" was a pet peeve of hers and my father's, though she was more stringent in scouring the dialect from my tongue. "That way of speaking will only hold you back," she'd snap. Her expression soured when I'd blurt out, "Watcha doin', huh?"

"*What are you doing?*" she'd say, emphasizing each word.

"My orm horts," I'd say.

"*My arm hurts,*" she'd correct.

Alice and my mother were both fair-skinned Creole beauties, but Alice's personality—critical, detailed and highly organized—couldn't have been more different from my mother's earthy and childlike qualities. Alice, chic and fashionable, lived in high heels, even wearing high-heeled slippers around the house. Her deformed toes curled inward from gripping the soles of her shoes. Routine-oriented and strict, she had little patience for kid-type nonsense. Most of her nieces and nephews found her formidably frosty; so, recognizing that she was softer on me, they often used me as a go-between when they wanted something from her.

Along with insisting I use proper grammar, Alice enrolled me in an etiquette school called Sugar-and-Spice, for girls and boys. The lessons were held in the back room of a department store. My new etiquette skills came into play when I took a train journey with my grandma Gladys to New Orleans and met my great aunt Dolly for the first time. I recall my grandmother prodding me into my aunt's living room, where she waited to meet me in her easy chair. Aunt Dolly was a large woman, and she didn't walk around much. Not knowing what to do as she gazed intensely down at me, I fell back on my etiquette.

"I'm pleased to make your acquaintance," I said and curtsied.

Aunt Dolly shifted the bulk of her rotund body in her chair to peer speechless at me for a moment, before she tilted her head back and let loose a howl of deep husky laughter. "Well ain't you somethin' else, um-huh, my, my. Look at that baby. What else can she do?" she demanded to know of my grandma. "Do she sing and dance?"

When my grandmother opened my suitcase later that night, which Alice had packed, she found my clothes ironed, starched, perfectly folded and smelling of flowers. This left such an impression on my grandmother that for the rest of her life she spoke of my neatly organized clothes whenever she heard Alice's name.

Alice taught me to sit still with my hands held lady-like in my lap so I would not draw attention to myself when adults talked among themselves. Unlike my mother, she had no interest in being my friend, but acted as a parent in every sense. At night I slept with curlers in my hair to create the ringlets Alice adored. My dresses were either frilly and shiny or conservative and chic like hers, streamlined to fit my small figure.

While Alice groomed me to become the lady she hoped I'd be, I also spent long days at a Compton preschool. The bright and cheerful colors of the artwork hanging on the walls, the toys at our disposal, and the chirping voices of Sesame Street characters blasting from the TV were only superficial deviations from the dysfunctional home lives that many of the children came from, and the teachers' methods of dealing with us were unorthodox at best.

When a little girl bit my ear so hard as to draw blood, I ran crying to one of my teachers and to show her the assault.

"Bite her back," the teacher said.

I didn't want to, and when I turned squeamish over the matter, the teacher grabbed my attacker, pinned her arms to her sides and demanded I bite her ear.

When I sank my teeth into the squishy flesh of her lobe, the girl's screams of pain terrified me.

"Now, you see. She won't be doin' it agin," the teacher told me, satisfaction rounding out her words.

A drop of blood sprang to the girl's skin where I'd left the imprint of my teeth.

"You betta stop that cryin' before I give you sometin' to cry about," the teacher warned the screaming child. "And you can take your little black butt and go sit down on one a dem chairs inside."

During naptime, the boys often used the girls who drifted off to sleep for masturbation. Creeping from their mats, the boys dry humped their classmates. I never closed my eyes and never did a teacher halt this regular, repugnant routine.

An innocent game of cops and robbers in the schoolyard turned into a brutal reenactment of gang rape. Two of the boys wrestled my friend to the ground and yanked her legs open while a third mounted her, pumping away.

I can still see the whites of her eyes as her head thrashed from side to side while the little rapist tried to kiss her. I pounded the boy's head and back with my fists, trying to pull him off of her until he turned around and punched me in the face. No teacher came to our rescue.

On one of my last days at the preschool, a girl was whisked away in an ambulance, her eye punctured by a needle driven in by another girl who sat sulkily on a blue plastic chair, swinging her legs and waiting for her parents to pick her up.

Alice's nephews were affiliated with the Crips gang. Ranging in age from twelve to sixteen, they sported enormous afros and carried giant hair picks in their back pockets. The boys liked to roughhouse with me and their little sister, Danielle, throwing us about in the front room of their home. We'd bounce off the plastic-covered furniture and barely miss colliding with a shelf full of family photos and figurines or the big wooden TV set, which sat decoratively on the muddied green spongy carpet. With a wink or grin, they'd say, "Y'all Crips. Crip or die. Don't be talkin' Bloods 'roun' here. Who y'all?"

"Crips," Danielle and I mimicked.

At that, they'd hold out their hands and say, "Hey, giv' me five, giv' me five," and we'd all slap each other's palms.

Satisfied that we knew our place, the brothers took us to the corner store for ice cream. They preened and strutted before older girls, who gave them sassy looks and made sucking noises through their teeth to let them know they weren't all that. If a girl *was* interested, she'd swing her hips slowly from side to side when she walked away.

I stayed with Alice until she and my father began to argue over my care. At first Alice merely suggested the idea of adoption, testing his response. His flat out refusal meant the subject would be dropped for a while, but she couldn't let it go. Her constant nagging at his resolve only turned to bolder talk.

"She's my daughter now," Alice said one day.

I stood in the kitchen, sipping the nauseating obligatory glass of milk that Alice wanted me to drink every day. I heard her talking on the phone in the other room and knew better than to interrupt even though she was talking about me. Her voice took on the icy edge it had whenever something didn't please her.

"Her mother hasn't seen her in over a year," Alice said, "and you can't afford to take care of her, Jim. Who takes her to school every day, feeds her and buys her clothes? I'm the mother every day, Jim." Her voice dropped while she listened to my father, then she continued, "You can still visit her like you always do. Her mother's not around. Who knows how long she'll be in that place." Alice's voice grew softer. Whenever grownups spoke about my mother, it was always in a hushed voice. Conversation stopped altogether if they thought I was listening. I strained to hear more, but "the place" did not come up again.

I tried to imagine my mom and Synanon but only drew a blank. I didn't know what it was, and Theresa had faded in my mind. Alice's sister Stella once forgot herself and asked Alice, "Is it true the women don't have any hair in that place?"

No hair.

I could not paint a mental picture.

Synanon was a blank.

My mother was a blank.

No hair?

A few days after the overheard phone conversation, my bags were packed. Alice fussed over me while we waited for my father to pick me up and take me to his brother's, where I'd been told I was to live.

"You can come here any time, and I'll visit with you. You're still my little girl," Alice said, arranging my ringlets into the perfect Shirley Temple spiral curls that she loved. I had never before seen Alice flustered or with tears in her eyes.

My father showed up shortly, giving me a brief hug and Alice a breezy hello before he hefted the suitcases Alice had lined up by the door. We watched him as he made a few trips to place the luggage in the car before he came back to retrieve me. Alice bent down to give me a kiss on my cheek, leaving a residue of her perfume on my clothes. My father opened the door, and Alice followed us part of the way toward the car, her heels clicking on the cement.

"You take care of my daughter, Jim," Alice called out.

My father's hand tightened on mine, his jaw hardening. "Goodbye, Alice," he said. "Get in the car, Celena."

Once I was buckled in, we pulled away. Alice hadn't moved. Her brownish blond hair was pulled into a ponytail that accentuated the slimness of her face and the sad fatigue that had settled in her features.

At first I liked the idea of living at my Uncle Joe's. He had two children, my cousins James and Tammy, with whom I'd played during prior visits. We'd raced each other up and down the street with my father snapping pictures and sometimes arranging us in poses for the camera. When he could afford it, he took all three of us to an amusement park or movie.

My cousins' mother, Aunt Terry, was one of the few white people in the neighborhood. She always seemed delighted to see me, making a big deal about how pretty and smart she thought I was.

All this changed when I came to stay with them. I was squeezed into an already cramped bedroom with my cousins, a single mattress set on the floor at the foot of their twin beds for me to sleep on. Almost immediately Terry expressed her resentment of my living in her home.

The house was a small, boxy structure caged by iron bars that fitted the windows and front screen door. The interior embodied the decline of Aunt Terry's mental state. The sofa and easy chair were worn and sagging. The carpet was frayed. The stale odor from the cigarettes Aunt Terry and Uncle Joe chain-smoked never seemed to clear completely from the grayish air.

As a small child I had a habit of walking on my toes without realizing it, an idiosyncrasy my aunt particularly hated almost as much as she generally disliked me. In the early evenings before my Uncle Joe came home, she made me walk the length of the living room heel-to-toe with a clothespin fastened over my nose. I'd wait, keeping still with my head lifted toward her nicotine-stained fingers while she clipped the wooden pin on my nostrils, a cigarette dangling from her lips, limp brown hair framing her white, narrow face. "We may as well try and fix your nose. It's too wide. Practice your walk."

I took a few steps toward the front door, careful to keep the soles of my feet close to the floor. When she felt satisfied with my obedience, she'd sit on the sofa, inhaling smoke deep into her lungs, then letting it seep out of her nose and lips in flat thin wisps. "I don't want to see you on your toes tomorrow. Answer me when I'm talking to you, you little turd."

"Yes, ma'am." The wooden pin pinched my skin and made it hard for me to breathe. I focused on my steps and the faded brown carpet. I'd walk until my aunt grew tired of watching me and wandered off in her thin, pink terrycloth robe, the fabric balding in patches, the flap and scrape of her slippers emitting a tired sound.

The irony of her latent racism confused me. "You're an ugly little nigger. Too black," she often told me. Yet she'd married a man darker than I was. Because I'd experienced my mother's love and my father's and Alice's care and fuss over me, Terry's ailing mental health and the beatings she administered soon after I moved in never quite penetrated my essence. It was as if I had been emotionally inoculated. My aunt terrified me, yet I had the maturity to understand that she wasn't well.

Most days, Aunt Terry lived in her robe. Stagnation and boredom were advertised in the fat curlers she and other women in our neighborhood wore shamelessly to the supermarket along with bedroom garments they couldn't be bothered to change before they left the house. Their lives were one long day after the next. With their husbands gone to work, they had nothing to do but watch the soaps on TV and kids playing outside. And watch they did, their eyes heavy-lidded while they chain-smoked and drank endless cups of coffee.

Sometimes my cousin Tammy and I imitated our sluggish mentors. We sat on the twin beds where she and her brother slept, the beds posing as our houses. We'd pretend to talk on the phone to each other, our dolls drooped over our arms like babies.

"Girl, what choo fixin' to do?"

"Um-umh, dis baby be givin' me all kines trouble, girl."

Nighttime became my refuge. When Uncle Joe returned home after work, Aunt Terry didn't dare mistreat me. We sat down to dinner around the Formica table and ate pork chops, mashed potatoes and peas. Tall plastic cups of fizzy 7Up sat next to each plate.

My bald uncle, soiled with dirt from work, the grime thick under his fingernails, kept mostly to himself. Although I felt safer when he was around, his fearsome tough look scared me into keeping my distance. Eleven months younger than my father, Uncle Joe looked eleven years older.

My father maintained a trim figure, wore fashionable clothing and spoke in an elegant low timbre, rejecting the drawl of urban black speech in which consonants disappeared at the ends of words as though the speaker couldn't be bothered to pronounce all the letters. He mimicked the suave mannerisms and tone of his favorite Hollywood actors, Cary Grant and Rock Hudson.

Uncle Joe wore white tank tops, the fabric streaked with grease and straining across his hard, round belly. Tufts of hair shot out from the sides of his scalp, though the top of his head was smooth and shiny. At the end of a long day of work, he'd collapse into an easy chair and guzzle a few beers while having a smoke.

OVER THE COURSE of two years, my mother gradually receded in my mind to a ghostly shred of another time. She was no longer important in my day-to-day life. Then a phone call came in the middle of a winter afternoon.

"Your mother," Aunt Terry said, handing me the receiver. I reached for the phone, curious

"Hello?" I said.

"Hello, Celena? It's me. Your mother."

The voice sounded unfamiliar, a stranger's voice.

"How are you?" she asked.

"Fine."

"It's my birthday. I'm thirty years old today. What do you think of that?"

What did I think? Time had run away from us, but I was too young to process its passage. I had no words for the gay, bright woman on the other end of the line, her face blurry in my mind. Through the screen door I saw the neighborhood children riding their bikes.

"I don't know," I said.

I hung up without saying goodbye.

I hadn't stopped loving my mother. I just didn't see how she fit into my life. She had become an abstraction, the woman who went to "that place," the secret place adults spoke of in hushed voices, shooing me away so I wouldn't overhear something I shouldn't.

After a time, my father became suspicious about Aunt Terry. Maybe a neighbor dropped a hint. Perhaps his own intuition caused him to wonder.

"Tell me the truth," he said one afternoon, squatting before me so we were eye to eye. "Is your Aunt Terry treating you right?"

I stared at his earnest, handsome face.

"Sweetie, don't pick at your skin like that." He pulled my hand away from my arm.

I'd taken up the habit of digging my nails into my skin and peeling it off a little at a time.

My aunt stood behind my father. Fear crackled in her gaze, her lips tucked in tightly. Anxiety hung like a cloak around Terry whenever my father came around. It showed in her nervous smile and the steady stream of cigarettes like miniature lifelines assuaging her shipwrecked psyche. She seemed to sense his repulsion in the curt way he spoke to her and the flare of his nostrils. My father had a temper; several of his brothers did, too, and Terry had been on the receiving side of it more than once.

What was I to tell him when he waited for me to speak? Would he take me home with him that day and never bring me back to Aunt Terry's? I couldn't afford the risk that he might later change his mind and decide Aunt Terry's wasn't that bad after all.

"Celena," he urged.

I thought of the beatings she'd given me, the sharp edges of the plastic racetracks that belonged to her son slicing across my skin, and the alcohol she poured on to the cuts afterward that burned like cold fire. She'd laugh gaily at my screams.

Should I tell my father of the spiders she forced me to kill? Or the eggs she cooked, scrambling the dead insects into the goopy mess, and forcing me to eat them? The games she liked to play in which she pretended to desert me at Taco Bell or McDonald's?

"Go and get some napkins," she'd order me, smiling, her children grinning next to her in the family car.

When I wouldn't budge, her teasing smile would evaporate, a chilly hatred settling in her cold eyes. "I said, 'Go get some napkins.'"

Hoping she'd change her mind, I'd open the car door and do as she'd asked. When I returned to the parking lot, the car was always gone.

At five years old, I didn't know where I was, what my phone number was or when she might be back. Too afraid to ask for help, I'd stand and wait, a stack of napkins clutched in my hand. The asphalt of the parking lot seemed wide and vast, yawning out to the chunky sidewalks, the busy street and surrounding buildings an urban forest that I could not navigate. I could only hope she'd come back.

She always did, after a few long minutes, pulling the car up next to me, my cousins and her laughing at my terror-stricken expression.

One of them would open the door. "Girl, we're just playing with you."

I stared into my father's insistent gaze. I wanted to go home with him, but I had only one chance to get it right. If he didn't take me with him, Aunt Terry would have her revenge. So I lied.

"I like it here," I told him. I looked at my aunt as her shoulders sagged with relief, a great puff of smoke floating from her mouth.

She smiled. "I told you, Jim. Everythin's fine. We love havin' Celena." The drawl of each word was as silky as ribbons.

My father watched me, the deep crease of a V between his brows. He didn't believe us. He rose to his feet as if he were being pulled against his will by an invisible string.

"All right," he said, turning around to face my aunt. "I'm warning you, Terry. If I hear anything, I mean anything, about you mistreating my daughter, you're going to hear from me."

Aunt Terry nodded. Her hand shook slightly as she took another drag from her cigarette.

Finished with her, my father led me out of the house and to his car for another outing to the movies.

In an effort to seem motherly, Terry followed us out and stood on the porch, waving goodbye. She leaned against the railing, her slender figure in bell-bottoms and a knitted top. Large sunglasses covered half her face. Many years later, when I saw a picture of her in a family photo album, I was surprised at how pretty and young she'd been during the time I'd stayed with her.

After that brief encounter with my father, she curbed her abuse quite a bit. The beatings grew less frequent.

I began to spend the bulk of my time with my father's mother, who lived across the street from Aunt Terry. A quiet woman, little more than five feet tall, my grandmother kept busy with her domestic routines. Cleaning her house, gardening, sewing and cooking took up all her time. She wore simple dresses adorned with aprons, a style reminiscent of her many years as a farm wife in Louisiana. She'd raised nine children in a small house while her husband worked in the fields, growing cotton and other agricultural products. Kerosene lamps provided light when it was dark; an icebox kept food cold, and my father milked the family cow every morning. Television had not yet infiltrated their home. Superstitions were rampant. It was a far cry from South Central Los Angeles.

My grandmother had never been to school. She had never learned to read, write or drive a car. In all my life, I had seen her as a passenger in a car only twice. She grew up speaking Creole, broken French, giving her English a blunt, clipped accent. For all that, she was practical and hardworking. I felt cared for at her home, a refuge from my unraveling aunt.

In the fall of 1976, I started first grade at a four-story Catholic school. I was proud to finally be a big girl, my Catholic school uniform a banner of proof.

The following February, I was kidnapped.

CHAPTER EIGHT

The Kidsnatchers

IT WAS night when she came for me. Her shorn head, large hoop earrings and jean jacket were non-identifiers. She came with a friend. They were clearly a pair, dressed the same. When my uncle Danny, whose home I'd been visiting over the weekend, opened the door, my cousins and I fell silent, sensing danger.

Were they here to rob us? I thought my uncle would slam the door in the women's faces, lock it and call the police, but instead he invited them in.

They sat on the couch. Aunt Rosa offered them coffee while Uncle Danny talked to them as if they were normal people.

We children scuttled into the hall, peeping around the corner at this bizarre intrusion. Who were they?

The leaner one dipped her head, rested her index finger against her temple, propped her elbow against the armrest. A familiar movement.

Little by little I began to recognize her, the jaw line, the chin and the timbre of her voice, silvery, gentle. I came out from my hiding place, a little closer and a little closer, until I reached out and touched her arm. "Excuse me. Are you my mom?"

The adults continued their conversation.

"Excuse me. Who are you? Are you my mom?"

She turned toward me. "So, you've finally recognized me. Yes, I'm your mother."

"And I'm Mary Ann," the other woman said, her cheeks indenting into deep dimples.

They both smiled, and I realized they were not as scary as I'd first thought. My mother rested her hand lightly on my shoulder. "I've come to get you," she said. "I've come to take you to Synanon. Would you like to go to Synanon with me?" Her tone implied fun, like when my father said, "How 'bout we go see a movie?"

I had not seen Theresa in more than two years, and at six years old I couldn't fathom why she'd shown up dressed the way I imagined a murderer or someone who rode around on a big noisy motorcycle might look. What was Synanon? I knew it had something to do with her, the place she'd gone off to. I'd never thought of Synanon as a place I could visit. Rather, I thought of it as a secret.

Catching the excitement in my mother's voice, my younger cousins, barely older than babies, ran up, no longer afraid of the bald women. They grabbed my hands and jumped up and down, yelling, "Yeah, we're going to Synin."

"No. No." Aunt Rosa pulled our hands apart. "Only Celena," she said in her accented English. She physically prodded me out of the living room and down the hallway to my cousin Donna's room, where I'd left my small suitcase when I'd arrived earlier in the day. My cousins followed us, watching silently while I retrieved my overnight case and my favorite doll, a Baby Alive from Toys "R" Us.

A short time later, I left my aunt and uncle's home with my mother and Mary Ann. I sat in the back seat of their car while Mary Ann drove and the two women talked to each other, the headlights from the traffic glinting off their earrings. I fell asleep, and when next I woke, we'd arrived at our destination. We stepped from the car, and I clutched my stranger mom's hand as we walked across a desolate street to a large, rundown building. Trash fluttered across the sandy, cracked sidewalks. The air was cold and laced with the salty scent of the nearby ocean. Only later would I learn that we'd stayed at the old Casa Del Mar Hotel, owned by the Synanon community in Santa Monica, California.

We entered the hotel through double doors into a dimly lit foyer. The carpet, faded and old, displayed an obsolete grandeur. We went up a short, winding staircase to a vast room. A single massive strobe light hung from the high ceiling. Most of the other lights were out, and a few people, bald like my mother and her friend and dressed in overalls, moved about the room, tidying up.

"Sit here," my mother said, guiding me to one of the long wooden picnic tables and benches that took up the middle of the room. "I'll be right back."

I did what I was told, watching as she hurried to the shadowy perimeter of the room and disappeared around a corner. Minutes later an overall-clad woman approached me with a bowl of red Jell-O.

"Here you go," she said.

I perked up, took a bite, then set down the spoon in surprise. An acrid bitterness had flooded my taste buds, my first taste of a dessert made with saccharine, a popular sweetener in the commune. I pushed away the bowl and waited for my mother to return.

Some parents who found it difficult to negotiate with their ex-spouses and other relatives resorted to kidnapping.

My weekend visit in Riverside with my mother's brother, Danny, had been part of a Kidsnatcher plot, which her brother had agreed to go along with. I was taken on a Friday night, but my father would not learn of my abduction for two days. Sunday evening he received a call from my aunt Terry, who was in hysterics.

"Celena's gone, Jim. She's gone." And that was all my father could get out of her for the first minute or so.

"What do you mean 'she's gone'?" he said. "Someone took Celena?" My father later told me that he'd never felt such a cold fear in all his life as the time he received that call. At first he thought a stranger had snatched me. Once Terry calmed down, he was able to glean some information from her and realized the person he needed to talk to was Danny. When he spoke to my mother's brother, the friendliness in my uncle's voice, when he had called my father a few days before to invite me to visit at his home, was gone.

"Aren't you out of work? Wouldn't Celena be better off with her mother in Synanon if you can't look after your daughter?" Danny interrogated him.

My father shook with rage. "I would never take your kids and give them to some commune, no matter how hard you were struggling, Danny. How could you have sent my daughter off to a place full of ex-convicts and drug addicts, people like those Manson lunatics?" They exchanged a few more words before my father hung up and hopped in his car to drive to Danny's, where he planned to beat him senseless. On his way, he stopped at his mother's, my grandma Regina, who talked him out of it. What persuaded my father to not follow through with driving to Danny's was my grandmother's revelation. "Terry was beatin'

Celena somthin' fierce. Her screams could be heard up and down the street," she said.

My father had suspected something was wrong, but no one would tell him. He has often repeated that if he'd known, he would have taken me away from Terry's the same day. But he didn't know. His mother's disclosure left him deflated.

Later he went to see an attorney about getting me out of Synanon. The attorney told my father that he couldn't help him. He said, "Even if you were a wealthy man, I'd have a hard time getting your daughter out of there. Synanon is a powerful organization with a tremendous amount of money to fight the case. They have their own lawyers, who work around the clock for free. Then there's also the fact that your daughter's mother has custody. There are other families in your situation who are fighting Synanon, and the cult has turned violent, so much so that a lot of attorneys don't want to go up against the place. It's probably best to wait until her mother gets tired of Synanon and leaves on her own."

My father tried to call the Synanon headquarters in Marin, but was stonewalled. He couldn't get my mother or me on the phone. He had no better chance of contacting us than if we'd taken a spaceship to the moon.

CHAPTER NINE

Assimilation

I STOOD on the porch of the Commons, hugging myself against the cold. The building had been empty of diners for some time. A rolling fog traveled over the landscape as if sentient, giving the appearance of unfurling the three small boys who approached. I'd been in the commune long enough to know they were from the Hatchery, a separate building from the usual dorms, where children lived from birth to age three or four. Demonstrators maintained the building and cared for the children. I watched the boys walk toward me and climb the steps to the porch.

We stared at each other, their eyes gazing along the length of my body.

I crossed my arms as two of them circled me.

Without a word, they jumped me, punching my body and grabbing my arms while I struggled to stay on my feet. One of them got his small hands around my throat. His lips twisted into a grimaced smile. Panicked, I hit his face. He fell back while the other two continued to attack me. Swinging wildly, I tried to make contact with a body.

I wasn't sure what made them stop, but they pulled away as if part of some orchestrated, sinister dance. They departed just as they had arrived, and I watched them climb down the steps with their short baby legs and walk into the mist, the blue of their overalls a smear of color in an otherwise colorless landscape.

Stunned, I tried to regain my breath as I pulled my jacket tighter around me and left the Commons, heading for the safety of the bunkhouses.

I didn't tell anyone what had happened. There was no one to tell. I had no parent, no close friend and no sense of connection with the demonstrators. It had been a month, perhaps, since Theresa had left me at the school, and I was still trying to make sense of the world into which I'd been thrust and left to navigate on my own.

It seemed that every other day I met someone new. One day, a girl with her arm in a cast sat outside my bunkhouse and asked me how I liked being in the school. She'd been aware of my existence. I couldn't say the same for her.

On another day I sat on a beanbag in the living room and watched as another child I had never seen before ran into the room, howling in pain.

"What happened?" the demonstrator supervising us asked, hovering over the girl and looking for the issue. "Do you want a rice cake?"

I perked up at the word "cake," hoping we'd all get a slice.

The demonstrator left, and when she returned, she held a plastic bag of what looked to me like Styrofoam disks. I wondered where the cake was. The demonstrator pulled out one of the disks and handed it to the girl, who bit into it.

"Celena, do you want a rice cake?" the demonstrator asked.

She held out the bag to me.

When I hesitated, she rummaged inside it, pulled out a second disk and gave it to me. I took a bite, unsure, and tasted nothing, my mouth filling with the puffy texture. I decided it was not food, walked outside and when I thought no one was looking, tossed it into the bushes.

On weekends, the hawkish attention that the demonstrators paid to the children diminished to almost complete disinterest. Each Saturday and Sunday for the first several months in the commune, I wandered the property of Walker Creek, often on my own.

In those early days I also explored my immediate surroundings: the cluster of bunkhouses and other buildings that made up the children's quarters. One building held a series of playrooms, each named for the color of its walls—Orange Room, Green Room and Blue Room. Leading to these rooms was the Reading Room. There were also storage rooms in the bunkhouses, which held piles of dolls, stuffed animals, baby strollers, blankets and the like.

One afternoon I followed the narrow, paved road that wound through the property and saw a rare sight: a moving car.

I found a yard full of every imaginable kind of tile—some stacked neatly, others tossed in messy, mountainous heaps on wooden pallets as far as I could see. I explored the tile yard for an hour or so, winding my way through the maze of multi-colored ceramic and porcelain materials and never saw another person. Nor did I ever see anyone there in subsequent visits.

I found other places like the tile yard, buildings two or three stories high, barn-like structures with tin roofs. Layers of dust and dirt covered every surface inside them. Cobwebs hung in dusty tatters or curtained the corners, shimmering expansively at times. These buildings were bursting with various items: clothes, shoes, blankets, record players, records, cabinets, dining tables and chairs, all stacked haphazardly or packed in boxes. I spent hours sorting through things, playing records and trying on musty-smelling clothes before some of the hazy mirrors. Light poured through the windows, making visible the dust particles that swirled through the air, giving the spaces a ghostly feel.

On another walk, I discovered an old speedboat in the middle of a meadow and, not far from the boat, a decaying cow and calf. The calf was just bones with bits of skin and fur, but the cow was mostly intact. Its stomach had expelled a pool of white, foul-smelling goop teeming with maggots. I went back to look at the bovine corpses every weekend until the cow was nothing but scattered bones.

Some of the other girls introduced me to the children's zoo, which consisted mostly of rabbits kept in individual hutches that sat high above the ground on stilted wooden legs. I had to stand on a two-step ladder to open the hatch door. I was allowed to pet the velvety fur of the skittish creatures, but warned to never touch the tiny pink newborns because the mother might kill them if she smelled an unfamiliar scent on their smooth, bubblegum flesh.

Weekends were about autonomy. I might wander alone, set off on an adventure with another child or join a group of kids in a game of tag or Monopoly. Mostly I played on my own. Other than a brief friendship with a girl named Anna, who replaced my "buddy" Sophie, I did not yet have connections with any of the other children.

Anna, an older girl who was well liked by the demonstrators and other kids, treated me like a favored pet. During free times, I went everywhere with her. As her favorite, I found myself regularly fussed over, my cheeks pinched by other, older girls, who exclaimed, "Ahh, she's so cute!" When Anna left the commune, I once again became solitary.

Having no understanding of my situation and no firm grasp

of time during my first year at Synanon, I absorbed whatever was around me in the osmotic way young children do. I learned Synanon habits and behaviors and the cult's unique vocabulary.

WAM meant "walking around money," or allowance. Every week I received two shiny quarters, which could be spent at a makeshift store that opened for the children Saturday afternoons in one of the many playrooms. Fold-up partitions created a temporary space within which boxes of sugar-free carob bars sat on rectangular tables. There were also Corn Nuts, chips, gum and other snacks for purchase. A child nine years old or older ran the cash box while the rest of us browsed the goodies, not wanting to be hasty as there would be no more treats until the following Saturday. Some children chose not to spend their WAM, but were instead champion savers. They gave up the little store full of snacks to stash away their quarters in ever bulging envelopes. Their main enjoyment was counting their growing savings.

When personal standards slipped, we received a "pull-up," a sharp rebuke, which could come from anyone, even another child. A grumpy face or bed with sloppy hospital corners could result in a pull-up. The person who received it was expected to reply with a rigorous "thank you very much" to the person who had taken the time to deliver the reminder.

"Act as if" was an attitude we were constantly reminded to adopt. If we didn't like something, we were to act as if we did. Smile and eventually we'd supposedly learn to like it.

The busy weekly routine and my exploratory weekends kept me from dwelling on the fact that I had not seen my mother since she'd brought me to Synanon. Once again, life took up my attention. My mother and family were relegated to the occasional thought.

CHAPTER TEN

A Visit

"YOU HAVE A LETTER."

One of the many demonstrators who looked after the children placed a slim pink envelope in my hand.

I stared at it, surprised. Every week, mail arrived for my peers, but I'd never thought there would be a letter for me. I went to my shared bedroom and sat on my bed, where I opened the mysterious envelope. It contained a single sheet of paper with pretty writing.

My Dearest Celena,

How are you? How do you like living in the school? I miss you every day.

Right now I am living in a city called San Francisco with other Synanon members. I am working hard to come and visit you. Soon I will have a chance and we can spend the day together. Any

time you would like to speak with me, you can write me and I will be sure to get your letter.
I love you, your mother, Theresa

I read the words over and over again. She was coming to see me? When? I carefully placed the letter with my other personal things in my end-table drawer.

It was Saturday morning, and I heard the blare of television cartoons from the living room. We did not watch much TV. Weekends were the allocated time, and sometimes we watched one or two shows during the week.

I closed the door to the bedroom, hoping to have a moment to myself. Sitting on my bed, I drew my knees up to my chest and thought about my mother for the first time in a while.

Physically, we were very different. The first time I had taken notice, I had been three years old, the age at which young children begin to emulate their parents' mannerisms, speech patterns and intonations. Standing in our bathroom, I had watched in the mirror while she'd brushed her hair, the bristles gliding easily through the silky brown waves, which cascaded over her shoulders.

My own kinky hair popped out from my head in short little bushes of frizz that refused to obey the motions of my imitation grooming, refused to lay flat and smooth like my pretty mother's. The harder I brushed, the puffier my hair became, until I had a halo of brown cotton candy. Angrily, I pressed down one side, crying out my frustration while my mom watched me, amused. To appease me, she braided my hair into several chunky plaits, fastening the ends with colorful plastic barrettes.

Shortly after I got the letter, I received a large doll. The present astounded me, as the idea of presents was far removed from my new reality.

"It's from Theresa," the demonstrator said.

This information was as stupendous as the gift itself. I was still trying to make sense of the school at Synanon. When I'd first arrived, all my personal possessions had been confiscated, and not long after I'd been introduced to the communal playrooms. At first I did not know children could own things; however, later I learned that all children possessed personal belongings. The doll was still sealed in its tall box, its blank eyes staring at me through the clear plastic. I quickly opened it, releasing the hard plastic limbs from the twist ties that held them in place. Some of the girls who had been around me when the gift arrived stood and watched.

"Ahh," they cooed, once I had the doll out of the package.

I let them pull the shiny brown springy curls and touch and stroke the bright yellow dress. The doll had brown skin like mine and curls just like I had. I loved her at once and even more so because she came from my mother, who had reached celebrity-like status in my mind compared with the utilitarian demonstrators and their evenhanded, often emotionless treatment of the other children and me.

Later that morning I walked with my new doll up the road to the Commons for breakfast, which extended into brunch during the weekends. In the distance I saw a familiar figure. I stopped, squinting into the sunlight, unsure. The woman walked toward me, but didn't seem to notice me. I tried to make out her features.

Was she my mom?

I called out, "Theresa!" to her and waved.

She still didn't see me, but she heard my greeting because she hesitated, looking around and over her shoulder.

I waved again.

Finally she saw me and waved back with such enthusiasm that I knew she must be Theresa.

I ran to her, hindered by the giant doll banging against my legs and threw myself into my mother's open arms. We embraced and I felt I might explode with the kind of joy a child feels when she's awakened to find Christmas has arrived with all its pleasures.

"I got your present," I said, once she had released me.

"It is not from me, sweetheart. It's from Grandma."

"Oh!" I felt even happier to know that other people in my family knew where I was, that I hadn't been forgotten.

Kneeling, Theresa took my hand, her greenish eyes assessing me.

"Isn't it funny," she said, "that we ran into each other when I was on my way to come visit you? We have the whole day together, just you and me. Where were you going?"

"To breakfast."

"Would you like to come and have breakfast with me in the Shed?"

I nodded, excited to be with my real mom and eat at the buffet-style setup where I could choose what I wanted instead of the usual powdered milk and soupy scrambled eggs with toast served in the Commons.

The Shed, a large block building with corrugated metal siding, housed the adult dining room. It was a sprawling space divided into smaller sections that were reserved for VIPs, who dined at round, café-style tables draped with tablecloths and set with linen napkins and sometimes fresh flowers or candles as the centerpiece. Everyone else ate in the larger dining hall at long, plain wooden tables that seated four or more people.

"How do you like the school?" Theresa asked while I walk-skipped alongside her.

"I want to live with you," I said.

"That would be fun, wouldn't it?" She stopped and looked around. We were alone on the country road, which ran through the center of the property, yet Theresa lowered her voice. "I'm working on trying to come here and be a demonstrator in the school. Then we could see each other every day. Wouldn't that be nice?"

"Yes. But when are we leaving?" Naively, I thought the long strange visit was now coming to an end.

She laughed and hugged me to her. "When we're finished eating, I have a surprise for you."

In the Shed, we each took a plate from the stack of dishes ready for use by the buffet and served ourselves. We sat at one of the long wooden tables.

I watched as Theresa stabbed one of her potatoes and popped it into her mouth, chewing loudly, and dipped her buttered English muffin into the thick goopy mess of the sunny-side up eggs. Some of the yolk dripped onto her fingers, which she licked efficiently, making a sharp sucking sound.

She wore a colorful silk scarf on her head and gold hoop earrings. When she glanced my way, we smiled at each other.

"Aren't you hungry?" she asked.

I hadn't eaten much, unable to take my gaze away from her. It was if she were an apparition and might disappear at any moment. I took a bite of muffin, savoring the chewy sour bread and rich taste of butter.

The sounds of people playing the game filled the room from the Wire, a dedicated Synanon radio station. I had grown used to the noise and learned to block out the intense talks, screaming and cussing, a kind of ubiquitous vocal demolition derby.

My mother's visit lasted part of a day. I remember little of it other than strolling hand-in-hand with her through a plant nursery near the Shed, the walk back to my dorm and the surprise she'd mentioned when we'd encountered each other on the road. She presented me with several Golden Books and read them to me in my room while I snuggled against her body, pressing my cheek against her soft breast, everything feeling right again.

After the last story, Theresa set the shiny, hard cover books in a small stack on my nightstand. "I have to go now," she said. She frowned at the books, tracing one of the golden spines with her index finger.

I pushed myself up and wrapped my arms around her neck. She hugged me and made to pull away, but I clung to her arms. "I want to stay with you. Don't leave me."

Gently she pushed my hands away. "I will come back and visit. We can write letters. Do you know how to give an Eskimo kiss?"

"No. What's that?"

She bent down and gently rubbed the tip of her nose against mine. "That's an Eskimo kiss, and this is a butterfly kiss." She brought her face closer, blinking so I could feel the flutter of her eyelashes against my cheek.

I grabbed her pretty face and repeated the Eskimo and butterfly kisses.

"I love you," she whispered.

It would be months before I saw her again.

CHAPTER ELEVEN

B^{etty}

NO DEMONSTRATOR BANGED a cowbell in the doorway. When I glanced at Sophie's bed, it was empty, unmade, the blankets in a twisted jumble. Slices of light cut through the Venetian blinds, creating bars of shadows on the opposite wall. The sun had risen, but no one had bothered to wake me for the start of the school day.

Slipping from my bed and stepping gingerly onto the carpet, I heard movement and quiet talking. When I poked my head out of my room, though, I found the hallway empty. The hushed voices seemed to come from the living room.

I wandered over to the communal area, pausing at the entrance. Everyone who lived in the bunkhouse sat huddled on the floor or a beanbag, listening to the Wire. A few demonstrators, their eyes red-rimmed and blurry with tears, stood over the radio listening to a man speaking in a sober tone. They leaned toward the box the way people do when the news is important.

A child passed me in her nightgown. "What happened?" I whispered.

"Betty died," she said, tucking her head and scurrying to join the others.

The idea that someone who wasn't in a movie could die was a startling thought to me. I had no idea who Betty was, but I didn't say so because it seemed that I ought to know. I imagined she must be one of the children in the school.

Gradually, over the course of the morning, I gained little bits of information. She had died of lung cancer. I didn't know what lung cancer was.

The mournful atmosphere peaked an hour later when a little girl emerged at the top of the dorm's second floor, her eyes blurred with tears, the skin around her nose ringed red. A demonstrator ran up the stairs to embrace her and stroke her dark head.

"Oh, Leda, I'm so sorry," the demonstrator said.

The attention only made Leda cry harder. When the demonstrator pulled away, the girl's eyes rolled toward the ceiling and she grabbed the banister, swaying slightly. The scene was very dramatic, and I felt out of place watching in my nightgown as if I were in someone else's home witnessing what should have been a private moment.

I didn't remember ever seeing Leda before. Like so many of the kids, she came into existence, for me, seemingly out of nowhere. I later learned that she had been close with Betty, that Betty was the founder's wife and that Leda was his grandchild. I didn't know what "founder" meant.

Someone mentioned Chuck.

Chuck.

Did I know Chuck?

The name seemed familiar.

We were given little booklets with a picture of Betty and Chuck on the front, and I recognized them from various framed pictures displayed throughout the premises. Chuck was a big, fat man with a dark pelt of graying hair and one eye smaller than the other. He always seemed to be in mid-sentence or glowering at the camera. Like everyone else, he wore bibbed overalls.

An enlarged picture of Betty and Chuck hung in my bunkhouse. She wore a white dress with a high neck and lace collar. A silk hat adorned her bald head, and her thin arm was linked through her husband's, who, for his part, sported a white suit. Betty's black skin contrasted sharply with Chuck's pale tones, making them appear to be negatives of each other.

Until that morning I'd given these ubiquitous framed pictures no thought at all. They were merely part of the backdrop of the surroundings in which I'd been placed, blending in with the aseptic environment of the dormitories, cookie-cutter uniforms and shorn heads.

In the days that followed, our time became a dedication and ongoing memorial for a woman who, I learned, had been much beloved and powerful within the community. Stapled booklets of her thoughts about good Synanon living were assembled and handed out for people to read. Her famous quotes were often repeated, as was the story of a bird that perched on her bed during her final moments, the notion being that the bird was a messenger that had come to take her away. This peculiar tale and the fact that she was often referred to as "The Magic Lady" fired my imagination.

The demonstrators used Betty's death as an opportunity for a teaching marathon about Synanon history and Betty's importance to the community. During their impassioned speeches and home movies of past Synanon events, some of the commune's rituals came to be explained to me. Betty had once been a prostitute and drug addict. I'd heard the term "drug addict" before, and I knew that many of the adults at Synanon as well as some of the demonstrators who took care of the children had been drug addicts or prostitutes. I hadn't a clear idea what these things meant, only that they weren't good.

Chuck, the demonstrators preached, had saved everyone in Synanon from the wretchedness of their previous lives. "If it wasn't for Chuck," the demonstrators lectured, "the whole lot of us would be basket cases, rejects of society. Chuck developed the game to help people get their anger out and become new men and women who could have some self-worth. We all have a lot of anger eating away inside of us, even children; that's why playing the game is important. In the game people release their festering feelings, feelings that are poisonous to their development."

Betty had come to Chuck for help in the early days of the community, when he was curing people in his living room. She'd been a raw trembling mess, strung out on drugs, spewing her rage and hatred of the world. No one had to teach her how to cuss. She knew all the bad words and wasn't stingy with them. I imagined her as a wild-eyed woman with hair standing on end, legs spread in a fighter's stance and hands on her hips while she yelled and screamed at others, who I envisioned cowering in their game chairs. Betty had come to Chuck wild from the streets, but his therapy had tamed her because he was a brilliant man, I learned.

Community members considered Chuck and Betty's marriage to be a beautiful symbol of racial equality. When demonstrators spoke of their union, they used the term "racially integrated couple."

During Betty's ongoing memorial, I also learned how Synanon had adopted the ritual of cutting off all its members' hair. It had started with a bakery and a steel beam built too low. When Chuck inspected the new building, he banged his head on the metal when he walked under the beam. Outraged, he demanded to know which idiot had made such a stupid mistake, and he immediately called for the man who'd created such a poor design to step forward, claim responsibility and have his head shaved. Men who fell into disfavor with the founder or a VIP shaved their heads as punishment. Woman who offended wore a stocking cap.

A few men took responsibility for the shoddy design and shaved down; however, others who had been on the construction crew also believed the low beam was their fault. Before long the whole crew had shaved heads. Other men in the community who had nothing to do with the construction decided they, too, ought to stand by their brothers. Within a matter of days, all the men had shaved their heads.

Until then, the massive head-shaving extravaganza had been a cleansing camaraderie for the men, yet when the women discussed doing the same, many of the men were appalled and spoke out against it. But once the first woman had started it, the rest followed. The children were next; however, they weren't such willing participants. Adults had to run after them and bring them, kicking and screaming, to the grooming stations.

With my peers, I watched one of the many home movies that depicted the first wave of head shavings amid a party-like atmosphere. One man shaved only half his head and beard, turning from side to side and laughing before taking all the hair off. Newly bald men and women danced to live music, which provided a jubilant backdrop to the mayhem of head shavings.

Further into the film, three lean, slick, shiny-headed women, one of them Betty, call a meeting. They giggle garishly, banging their hands on a table to get the attention of their equally bald audience.

We went over and over the same information: Betty's courageous, fierce personality and the love she and Chuck had for each other. Tears. Poems. Movies again and again. This went on for weeks.

Although I never met Betty, I began to envision her as a kind of angelic figure. In Theresa's letters, she expressed a high regard for Betty, who had inspired my mother through regular written correspondence to keep faith in bringing me to Synanon.

"She always responded when I wrote to her," Theresa told me. The passion and fervor of Theresa's feelings toward Betty seemed to spill from the pages of her letters.

Yes, I decided, Betty had been a special woman. My young mind marinated in images and talks of her saintliness; I wished I could have met her. I could not have thought any differently.

Once the Betty blitz wound down, we returned to our regular routine and talk of The Magic Lady dwindled.

One day, not long after Betty's death, the other children and I were told after inspection to wait outside our dorm instead of walking to the Commons. We stood for minutes in the crisp, cold air. I shoved my hands in my jacket pockets to stay warm.

The demonstrators responsible for our dorm emerged. One of the women walked behind a small boy with reddish-orange hair, her hands on his scrawny shoulders. She smiled widely in an I'm-making-a-point-here way. The boy, whose name I knew to be Santiago, looked toward the ground.

"This is a very special day," the demonstrator said. "Santiago woke up to a dry bed." She glanced down at him, the exaggerated smile never leaving her face. "When we put our mind to it, we can overcome our bad habits. Good job, Santiago!"

His pale cheeks blossomed to a ruddy red.

The demonstrator wasn't finished. "Everyone should know about and celebrate your success." She brought her hands together, methodically clapping, the loud, hollow, echoic sound breaking the quiet of the morning.

Santiago's head drooped. I wondered why the demonstrator didn't notice how much she was embarrassing him.

"Stand up straight," the demonstrator said, motioning for us to join her clapping.

We clapped long and hard while Santiago remained in his stiff stance, his brown eyes glazed and focused on some distant object.

Finally the clapping died down, and the demonstrated patted his shoulder. "Congratulations!" she said. "You're all excused for breakfast."

As we walked to the Commons, I watched one of the boys elbow Santiago in the ribs. "Yeah, congratulations, dork," the boy hissed.

Some of the other boys overheard this remark, and a dry laughter erupted from the group as they jostled one another, grinning hard as if to prove they were better than Santiago. Several of them had the same problem and lived on a floor dedicated to habitual bedwetters. The stench of urine clotted the air of their hallway like an unwanted badge of their inability to control themselves.

While most of the kids who suffered from this problem managed to wake up now and then with dry sheets, Santiago never had until that morning. Because of that he'd become the scapegoat for the other bedwetters' pent-up humiliation. Santiago had all the strength of a limp noodle and never bothered to defend himself, though he was often physically attacked by bigger boys who grabbed his thin arms and twisted them around his back.

His strategy: wait it out.

Throughout breakfast and then in the classroom that morning, adults and children continuously came up to Santiago to congratulate him. The boys pumped his hand and said, "Way to go. Good job!" in loud voices.

Our first grade teacher Ginny didn't get caught up in all the hoopla of fussing over poor Santiago. Later that afternoon, when school let out and our class set off for physical education, she pulled him aside, waving the rest of us away.

I slowed and looked over my shoulder, watching her kneel down and offer him a stick of gum while she rubbed his back. My respect for her grew exponentially in that moment, and so when some days later Ginny made an announcement to our class, I was conflicted.

"Everyone," she said, "I have some really good news." Eyes shining, she clapped her hands to get our attention. "Something really wonderful has happened for me. I will be going on a date with Chuck, so I won't be here next week. When I get back, I'll tell you all about it."

I stared at her, mystified. Chuck was an old man. In the pictures I'd seen of him, he looked like he could pass for Ginny's grandfather. It didn't seem right. He belonged with the dead lady Betty everyone had been crying over, not my young, pretty teacher.

A girl raised her hand. "Why are you going on a date with Chuck?"

Ginny glanced around the room at our blank expressions. Her smile seemed to tuck itself into the corners of her mouth, disappearing. "Well, I was chosen. It's a great honor."

This was a lie, like the lie that we were beautiful with bald heads. Her words fell like soap bubbles, shiny, bobbing and bursting into nothing.

Ginny seemed as if she might say something else. Instead, she grabbed a piece of chalk and wrote the date on the board. She never returned to the school to tell us how the date went. Weeks later, she married the old man.

I never saw Ginny again except in pictures. Through the years, her figure became husky and thick. At times when I saw the scowling, fleshy-faced woman she'd become, aged far beyond her years and grossly out of shape, sitting on a motorcycle and wearing dark sunglasses, or when I heard her on the Wire denigrating one person, threatening another, I'd forget that she was the same kind, youthful person who'd been adored at the school where she'd once taught.

CHAPTER TWELVE

Changing Partners

I'D BEEN LIVING in Synanon six months when Theresa arrived for one of her irregular visits. She brought her new husband, Larry, and had made arrangements for the three of us to have an outing. The destination was San Francisco; our mode of transportation, a reserved Synanon car.

I was given a dress for the occasion, black with flowers printed on the cotton material, the hem ruffled just above my knees. Theresa wore a drawstring blouse, wraparound skirt and brown, knee-high boots. A pale pink silk scarf covered her short hair. The ever-present hooped earrings dangled from her lobes. She tittered and fretted over me while she got me situated in the back seat.

Larry watched silently, uttering only one sentence: "Are you ready to go, Theresa?"

Once we were on the highway, Theresa turned in her seat to

glance at me, her bottom lip tucked under her large front teeth, her face happy, excited.

Larry focused on the road.

"What do you think of my new husband?" Theresa asked. Her eyes twinkled at me, and I realized she expected an answer. I leaned forward so I could get a better look at Larry's taciturn profile. Theresa also examined him as if she were sizing up a pet she'd recently purchased and wasn't sure she'd made the right choice.

Larry was boring, I decided. The robotic Abraham Lincoln, my least favorite attraction at Disneyland, was more entertaining than Larry, who had inexplicably become part of my mother's and my life through their mysterious marriage, which I was just now learning of.

"Nice," I said.

My answer seemed to satisfy Theresa because she turned to face the road. "We just recently got love matched," she remarked.

"Oh," I said.

I knew love matched was the same as married. Their union was just another fragmentary incident for me, part of a string of sketchy situations that I'd come to accept in my short life.

Larry drove with one hand and rested the other on the seat. Theresa's fingers grazed his lightly. "I thought maybe we'd go to Fisherman's Wharf," he said, pulling his hand away to place it on the steering wheel.

We went to Fisherman's Wharf. The air smelled of the sea. Flocks of gulls glided on the wind current in the bright sky. Boats of various sizes bobbed in the marina. Other tourists like us strolled the walkway and creaking wooden wharfs.

Until that rare visit with my mother and her new husband, I had no awareness of the experiment that was going on at Synanon. The reform, called Changing Partners, consisted of mass divorce followed by remarriage to a new partner.

After Chuck Dederich took my young teacher Ginny to be his new wife, he wanted everyone in the community to start a new relationship. His first guinea pig was his daughter Jady. Having been displeased for quite a while with Jady's husband, Dederich began to pressure her to divorce and marry someone else in the community whom Dederich felt more suitable for upper management grooming.

With this first successful breakup, Dederich got other Synanon VIPs involved in divorcing and remarrying. As more couples followed suit, the ones who held out were pressured to leave their marriages and find someone new.

It's "no more trouble than casting off an old coat," Dederich told members who balked at this drastic request.

In the fall of 1977, Changing Partners became an official mandate. Whether members were happy with their present spouse or not, it was time to take a of leap faith.

"We are jumping," Dederich said, "from one nuptial or marital or romantic or erotic adventure to the next, from a platform of love rather than a platform of hatred."

He later told a reporter for the *San Raphael Independent Journal*, "I thought, wouldn't it be funny to perform some emotional surgery on people who were getting along pretty well."

Mass divorces were performed, followed by enormous wedding ceremonies called Love Matches of ten or more new partners vowing their commitment for a maximum of three years.

Because children did not spend much time with their parents, Changing Partners had little or no effect on us. It made no difference in our day-to-day routines and was not a part of our lives in any concrete sense. I imagined it to be similar to the head-shaving films I'd seen, a party-like event. Only this time everyone danced in celebration of the divorces and remarriages. I also thought maybe they'd run out of the best men when it was my mother's turn to choose. It turned out that I was not too far off the mark.

Years later Theresa told me she had not wanted to participate at the beginning, when the new regimen was still voluntary and there were a variety of possible husbands from which to choose. Instead, she'd watched from the sidelines, amused, thinking it just a passing phase. Once it became mandatory to change partners if married or if single find a mate pronto, men she might have considered had already been snatched up.

She was gamed incessantly for putting too much thought into the matter and aggressively hounded to pick from the men who were left. Each time she turned down a suggestion, the game became more vicious. She was being too picky, members shrieked. Who did she think she was? There was nothing special about Theresa, her status.

Backed into a corner, both she and Larry entered their relationship reluctantly. They were married in a ceremony with several other remaining couples. "I did not really want to marry him," Theresa told me years later. "He was a friend who I saw as more of a father figure."

Their pairing lasted one year.

CHAPTER THIRTEEN

A Friend

"NO! NO! NO!"

The sounds of someone pounding the wall stopped me.

I watched as a young girl, writhing in the grip of a temper tantrum, came into view. A demonstrator pulled at the girl's arms, which were twisted above her head, and dragged her body across the carpet. "I won't wear a dress! I won't!" While she screamed, she managed to free one arm, which she used to claw at the floor.

"Your mother's coming to visit, and you will put on a dress for her," the demonstrator said.

The girl's head flew back. Her body arched as she tried to dig her short nails into the demonstrator's wrist. Another girl returned to the room with three dresses, all of them ruffled and feminine. I wondered where they came from. A pink dress was held out as a sort of suggestion. The screaming girl—her name turned out to be Laurie—yanked the dress off the hanger, pulling at the neckline. Eyes bulging, she managed to tear some of the fabric while the other child wrestled it from her angry fingers. The demonstrator dragged Laurie the rest of the way down the hallway to her bedroom while the child who held the dresses followed solemnly behind.

I later learned the visit never happened because Laurie refused to put on one of the despised dresses that had been hanging, hidden, in the back of her closet. I wondered why the visit with her mother mattered, as we were constantly being told our parents were not important.

Anyone who knew Laurie soon learned that she was not only a tomboy, but believed that she was a boy and everyone had made a mistake in this matter.

"I have a penis," Laurie told me the day we were getting to know each other. Her dark eyes, framed by thick albino brows, held my gaze, challenging me to argue the point.

I didn't, and we became friends.

When Laurie was not riding horses, she would hoist herself on my back and pretend I was a horse. I didn't mind. This game gave me a sense of belonging, like we were a pair.

When Laurie showered, she wore a washcloth over her genitals, explaining that she didn't want us girls to see her penis. We all grew used to this eccentricity of hers, and it became normal to see her soaping herself while she held a washcloth over her private area.

During room rotations, a few times I wound up sharing a room with Laurie; I found it hard to fall asleep because she spent thirty to sixty minutes every night banging her head on her pillow until she fell asleep. The springs of her mattress creaked loudly in protest to the thump, thump, thump of her head. Sometimes I watched her, too distracted with the noise to close my eyes. Her arms rested straight against her sides while she sat on her knees, eyes blank, upper body rising and falling rhythmically with machine-like precision.

When I wasn't running through the hills of tall blond grass with other girls, pretending to be princesses while we sang in high-pitched voices, our heads covered in pink-and-blue-striped blankets from the Hatchery that we used as imitation hair, I pretended to be a boy with Laurie.

We looked no different from the boys. Elderly adults in the commune, most of them wandering around in a state of perplexity, a few of them in the early stages of dementia, having arrived under the custody of their grown children, would smile when they saw us, however strange we may have looked. Usually the old women would stop to ask, "Now, what are you, sweetheart? A little boy or a girl?"

In the summer, I ran about shirtless during playtime. As much as I loved to play with dolls and pretend to be a mother, I also learned to enjoy climbing trees and hunting for snakes. I thrilled in the freedom of riding my bike full speed down steep hills with my hands off the handlebars. I came to realize I was naturally strong, so I liked to arm-wrestle, challenging anyone who might accept.

Whenever I was asked what I wanted to be when I grew up, I would announce proudly, "A man. A big tall man." This did not seem impossible. Reality in my short life was so warped that it seemed anything could happen.

"WHERE IS YOUR BELT?"

It was dinnertime, and I stood before the door of the Commons, waiting for the demonstrator to give the okay that I could enter. She stood with folded arms, studying me from head to toe.

My clothes were clean; my shoes not terribly scuffed up.

There were no stains anywhere; however, I had not thought to wear a belt, nor did I remember being told that I must. I looked at my jeans and the empty loops around my waist. I wasn't sure where my belt was or if I even had one. I didn't recall having seen one in my wardrobe.

Every week I stood in line with other children to receive my allotment of clothing.

"Size?" a demonstrator would ask.

"Seven."

A stack of white t-shirts and mix of dark blue jeans and overalls would be placed in my hands from the size seven shelf. Sometimes I received an overall dress. Many of the children and adults possessed wide, brown leather belts with enormous brass buckles. Some adults wore a sliver dollar as a centerpiece in their buckles. It was a popular style.

"You cannot come into dinner without a belt," the demonstrator said. "Go and get it."

I stepped away from the building, watching other kids file through the doorway, my stomach grumbling.

"What are you doing?"

I looked up to see Laurie standing before me.

"I can't go into dinner," I said.

"Why?"

"I don't have a belt."

"Did you lose it?"

I shrugged, not sure. I was never really sure of anything anymore, and this situation was not the first time I'd dealt with arbitrary rules. Once a demonstrator had banned me from coming into my dorm in the evening because I wore nail polish. I did not know that nail polish was banned because we had acquired it from the staff in the first place. The polish remover was kept in the bathroom. I had had no choice that night but to stand in the muted light of the entryway for over an hour gnawing the polish off my nails.

Laurie peered behind some bushes. She wore her favorite cowboy hat and brown cowboy boots, presents from someone. Legs slightly bowed and sturdy in her dark blue jeans, she bent over to sweep her hand under a hedge. "Were you carrying it?"

"Maybe." At seven years old, this scenario seemed as plausible to me as any. I helped my friend search for the missing phantom item, looking about more bushes, scouting grassy areas.

"It might be by those trees," Laurie suggested.

We walked across the road to where a few trees lined the shoulder.

No belt.

"I think it might be over here," Laurie said, lifting some barbed wire to a fence that skirted the bottom of the sloping hillside. She squeezed through the gap, then, holding up the pointy sharp wire, waited for me to follow.

I ducked through, feeling doubtful. I didn't remember ever playing in that area, but Laurie forged ahead. Soon we were on a narrow foot trail that wound its way gradually up into the hills. When the trail faded, we waded through knee-high grass.

After a while I could no longer distinguish one direction from another. The land rounded out every which way, and the darkening sky narrowed our scope of vision until finally there was nothing to see. We trudged through a curtain of black, our only illumination a scant smattering of stars.

Every time I expressed any doubt, Laurie sighed and claimed in her husky voice that she knew where she was going.

My belt dilemma nibbled at the periphery of my mind. I wondered when I had ever walked thorough these hills before. I decided I hadn't and that we were lost. I was sure of it.

"No, we aren't," my companion barked back at me.

We walked on. Before the sun had completely sunk into the west, we came across a herd of cattle with several massively muscled bulls, their thick fleshy humps rising out of powerful shoulders.

After much urging, Laurie talked me into following her through the bovine convention, reassuring me in her I-know-best voice that they wouldn't hurt us, then taking off at a sprint when one of the tremendous creatures snorted through its wide wet nostrils and began to make its way in our direction.

I was not far behind her.

In the last of the ashy twilight she unbuttoned her pants, pushed them down off her hips and stood with her legs apart and hips thrust forward, letting loose a jet of urine from between her legs.

A cold fog fanned out around us before our final plunge into inky blackness. We had no jackets. I was cold. My legs were tired and my stomach cramped with hunger. In a late afternoon physical education session, I had performed one hundred sit-ups, thirteen pull-ups and a series of push-ups and leg raises and run two miles up a steep incline to several huge, domed, metal water containers. After the run there had been yet another hour of soccer and now this seemingly endless walk in the hills. As I followed the sounds of Laurie's footsteps I was sure we were hopelessly lost and I had never had a belt.

As we ascended another hill, a faint light lit up the sky in the distance. Curious, I walked a little faster, keeping closer to the brisk pace Laurie set. When we reached the top of the hill, I saw down below us a smattering of buildings. The dormitories looked familiar, yet they were differently arranged.

"We're at the ranch," Laurie said. "See. I knew where we were the whole time."

We skirted down a sandy footpath slippery with pebbles. The path led to a paved road frequented by a passing adult or two.

"Only adults live here," Laurie explained. "It's their dinnertime."

The scent of sausages and potatoes wafted through the air as we fell into step with others on their way for the last meal of the day. No one took any notice of us.

Inside the dining hall we each grabbed a plate from the stack at the buffet and loaded it up with roast chicken, sausage, beef, rice, potatoes, vegetables and dinner roles with tabs of butter.

Halfway through dinner, someone tapped me on the shoulder. A man and woman stood over us. "Who are you here with?" the woman asked.

"No one," Laurie said.

"How did you get here?" the man asked.

Laurie pointed at me. "We walked over the hills. We were looking for her belt." She shoved a bite of chicken into her mouth and chewed, oblivious to the adults' concern.

"You walked here from Walker Creek?" The man's mouth hung open. "But that's six miles. No one at the school knows you two are here?"

A flicker of uncertainty fluttered in my chest.

"Nope," Laurie said and took a long drink of apple juice.

"Hank, go and call the school," the woman said.

The man left, but came back shortly. "Fred's going to bring a jitney around and take these girls to the children's property."

We were allowed to finish our dinner before we were bustled into a white van. Tired from the long walk and huge meal, I buckled myself into one of the plush seats and was asleep within minutes.

The next I knew, I was shaken awake. Laurie and I climbed out of the van and walked to our dorm. No demonstrator waited to escort us back. The other children had already gone to bed. In my room, I removed my clothes, slipped into my pajamas, climbed into bed and fell back asleep.

CHAPTER FOURTEEN

E ducation

A FEW OF us were in the playroom, listening to records, reading and playing jacks when the door whisked open and one of the male demonstrators came through pushing a wheeled blackboard. Several other children followed behind him.

I set down my book.

"We need some chairs," the demonstrator said.

The children who had come in with him left to get the chairs.

Next he gestured at the rest of us in the room. "Wheel those partitions over here."

I stood and went to the back of the room, walking around the babies from the Hatchery, who lay napping on blue-and-white-striped blankets. We were instructed to set up the partitions so they separated us from the sleeping toddlers.

The children who had left to get the chairs came back

carrying two each and set them in a semicircle formation, the usual layout for our seminars.

The rest of us went to get more chairs.

When I came back, the demonstrator had drawn three circles on the blackboard with a word inside each circle.

After we took our seats, I sounded out the words silently to myself: eh-go, id, super eh-go.

The demonstrator stood with a ruler and pointed at one of the circles. "Who can tell me about the ego?"

A boy raised his hand.

"Okay, Brad. Stand up," the demonstrator said.

Brad rose to his feet, his overalls sagging in the back. He gazed at the blackboard. "The ego is—" He paused. "The ego—" Another pause. "It's like if you had this car and you wanted to drive it really fast, that's the id. The super-ego says you have to go really slow to be safe, but your ego lets you go a little bit faster because the ego is in the reality."

"That's close," the man said. "Who else can tell me about the ego?"

Cindy raised her hand.

"Yes! Cindy. Stand up."

She shot to her feet, hands on her hips. "The ego is our conscience?"

I mouthed the word "conscience" to myself.

"The ego is how we do stuff every day, the right stuff," Cindy said. "The ego knows it's not good to eat five cotton candies because the id would do that, so the ego lets you eat one even though it would be better if you had vegetables. The ego sometimes has to make deals with the id, but mostly we live in our egos. If you don't listen to the ego, you might feel guilty from the super ego. When we play the game, sometimes we speak from the id. Our id is deep inside us."

I stared at the bubbles on the blackboard, trying to understand the ideas. In my mind I conceptualized the ego and id as tiny magical creatures forcing people to do things like eat too much cotton candy or drive cars a certain way while the conscience was just a big black space. The lesson continued, but my mind drifted. I didn't understand what was being taught or why playtime had been interrupted to talk about the ego. I retreated into my own world, something I was becoming quite good at.

Some days later I sat in another seminar, this one officially part of our schedule for the day.

"You are the models for the future," the demonstrator said while she paced the room before us. "And I am here to demonstrate that. Right? Am I right?"

"Yes," we chorused.

"Are you lucky to be here?"

"Yes."

"Why are you lucky to be Synanon kids?"

Silence.

"Look how many brothers and sisters you have. Look how many parents you have. On the outside, kids have to live with their biological parents in the nuclear family, but we know here in Synanon that this isn't good for children. The parents in these families smother their children with their clingy affections. Here you have freedom, you have space, you can breathe. Synanon children are smarter and healthier than children on the outside.

"Do you know what this is?" She spread her arms wide. "It's an experiment, a working experiment. That's what I mean when I say you are the models for the future. One day everyone will want to come to Synanon. All of you were lucky enough to be the first."

During my time in the school, I came to see other children's parents as a kind of curiosity, their relationships a concept rather than a reality. Some parents visited now and then, most did not.

Some worked as demonstrators, although after a while, it was easy to forget that a demonstrator had a child in the school because the parents did not seem to have any special bond with their offspring. I knew which adults were the parents of which kids, and in most cases there was a strong physical resemblance, but that was where the relationship ended. Adults led completely separate lives from us.

One of our many father figures in the school was Don Leitner, who showed up at some point as a demonstrator. Short and stumpy-looking with limbs not quite proportioned with his torso, Don had thin lips that disappeared when he smirked, which was often, and small round eyes set unattractively close together.

I hated him. It seemed that whenever Don and I were in the same room, his sole purpose was to publicly humiliate me. My only relief from his malice was Sophie, whom he loved to torture equally.

By the time Don started working in the school, I'd grown tired of seminars and lectures that often made no sense. Forced to sit through so many games and talks, I created a detailed fantasy world, to which I'd retreat whenever the need arose.

Don immediately spotted that I was not paying attention. The first time he demanded that I recite back to him everything he had said during one of his meetings, I remained silent and miserable, embarrassed that I could remember nothing.

"You can't tell me anything? Why is that?" He waited.

I said nothing.

"I think you can't tell me because you're an idiot. Are you retarded, Celena? Are you a retard?"

I felt my body grow hot while he laughed out of the side of his thin lips, the rest of the kids joining in. "I don't like retards, Celena. Next time you better pay attention."

But I couldn't.

Every time Don spoke, my mind closed. Desperately I tried

to listen, but my heart beating in my ears took precedence over the words.

With him, it became a game. "Okay, let's see if the idiot picked up anything this time," he'd announce.

All eyes would turn to me while I sat as mute as ever. Sometimes I'd recite back fragments, trailing off after a bit and wondering why I couldn't remember what he'd said. Fortunately, I did not have to deal with Don often, as he was a male demonstrator and usually oversaw the boys' dorms.

Years after I left Synanon, the constant probing into my psyche by the school staff and greater collective of the commune took the form of nightmares. In my dreams, I lay on an operating table surrounded by doctors dissecting my brain and discussing among themselves what they found. It was clear, one of the doctors always concluded, that my brain was no good at all. They would need to insert something into it to improve my intelligence and keep track of my whereabouts.

The assassination of Theresa's role as my mother succeeded only in creating a deeper longing to see her and venerate the mother's role. I had no greater wish than to be with her and become a mother myself. By the close of my first year in the commune, I developed an all-encompassing desire to be in a nuclear family with a mom and dad and a hunger for traditional domesticity that was out of reach outside of the cult, and nonexistent within it. The TV show *Little House on the Prairie* put images to my longings, creating an idealized vision of American frontier life and later a deep desire for self-sufficient remote living.

Not all Synanon children experienced my intense want for family life. Some had been born into the commune or arrived as babies, spending the first formative years of their lives in the Hatchery. For them, parents were of little consequence.

The demonstrators, who were supposed to replace the role of

parent, appeared, disappeared, reappeared and dropped out of the school and were replaced by new demonstrators, suddenly on hand.

We children experienced this same randomness in our living arrangements through regular moves. I would live in one room for a while, and then move to a different room or different building, or another child would share my room, replacing the previous child. I also never knew what grade I was in because I usually found myself in two grades simultaneously.

Years later, when I read old archives of Synanon school logs at a UCLA library, I learned in an entry dated August 13, 1977, that there were forty-four members on staff. Twenty-one of them where younger than twenty-one and a need was expressed for older, more mature adults. Half of the demonstrators responsible for raising the children were barely out of puberty themselves. Many were recently reformed drug addicts.

Thirty-four of the demonstrators had work schedules that consisted of seven days on and seven days off. Three of the staff worked five days with two days off, or five days with nine days off, while seven of the staff worked a consistent schedule of five days a week with two days off. Looking back, I believe this inconsistent scheduling was another method to keep us children from becoming too dependent on our providers.

CHAPTER FIFTEEN

Back to Basics

I STARED at a small brown turd that floated in the toilet bowl.

"Is this yours?" Mary Sue said, gripping my shoulder.

I shook my head.

"Go sit down."

I turned around and sat on the linoleum floor of the bathroom with the other children while the next child was led up to the toilet to take a look and likewise deny responsibility for the little floating poop. The room was getting crowded, and a short line snaked out to the hallway, where another demonstrator, Linda, stood in the doorway, guiding kids in to make the pilgrimage.

"Well, somebody did this!" Mary Sue screamed, pointing her thick finger at the toilet.

Mary Sue was short with lumpy legs and wide hips. Her eyes were big and round. When she got in a rage, it seemed as if very little held them in place and they might dislodge and roll away. I found her personality jittery and unpredictable.

I had learned from Mary Sue when she was new on the scene and still excited about being a demonstrator that she and Theresa were good friends. As I grew to know Mary Sue better, it was hard for me to imagine her having anything to do with my mom.

When no one claimed the poop, Mary Sue changed her tone to well-modulated calm. "Whoever is guilty of this, step forward and admit it. We will have a talk about hygiene."

No one came forward.

"Okay. Fine. You can all just sit here for as long as it takes."

I scrunched up my knees and buried my face in my lap. I wished I'd been playing farther away from the bunkhouse when we were all rounded up.

The interrogation continued until there were no more children who hadn't looked at the turd in the toilet.

We sat in silence.

Linda left.

When she came back, Mary Sue left.

More kids were found and brought to the bathroom. It became even more crowded.

"We can sit here all day and all night," Linda said.

After an hour I noticed an uncomfortable feeling. My bladder was full and my feet numb from sitting. I inched my body against the wall to stretch my cramped legs.

"Sit your ass down!" Mary Sue shrieked at me. "No! No! Come here!"

I stood up and walked to Mary Sue, who looked bug-eyed again.

"You did this, didn't you?"

I shook my head.

"Yes, you did! Admit it! Doesn't your shit look like that?"

Obediently, I glanced down at the puffy, water-logged poop that was starting to fray, stringy pieces pulling away and sinking.

"No," I whispered.

Mary Sue shoved me back toward where I'd been seated. "We're going to get to the bottom of this," she said.

The long shadows of afternoon passed over us. The light grew dim. Afternoon turned to evening. The demonstrators became tired. They excused us, announcing that tomorrow we would return to back-to-basics mode.

Our walk to breakfast the next morning became a mandatory silent march. The lack of chatter with just the sounds of our shoes crunching gravel opened my ears to a stillness I'd never noticed before. Hearing a bird call now and then and a whisper of wind rifling through the leaves on the nearby trees, I think I would have enjoyed the silence had it not been a punishment. Instead, I felt stilted and unnatural, not sure how careful I should be in keeping noise out of my movements.

All our free time was confiscated in service of back-to-basics. We were told we'd been lazy. Not flushing the toilet had been the last straw.

As we marched in the sharp cold of morning, our two long rows were intersected by another group of marchers. The Punk Squad consisted of teens who had been in trouble with the law or sent to Synanon by families who felt they'd lost control of their child. Punks typically had a rabid aversion to Synanon and were notorious for acting out. They were monitored closely, had little freedom and lived a near-constant military lifestyle. Punks wore overalls like we did, but instead of tennis shoes, their feet were clad in sturdy military boots.

The Punks marched uniformly through the mists in two parallel lines, breaking the quiet with their military singing, heads erect, eyes forward, arms swinging in unison. Their booted feet struck the ground all at once, defiant to our own silent progression.

Together, they sang, "There was a girl who wore a yellow ribbon. She wore it for her sweetheart who lived in Tomales Bay."

"Tomales Bay!" the girl's voices rang out.

The boys' baritone voices echoed, "Tomales Bay!"

"She wore it for her sweetheart who lived in Tomales Bay!" They marched strong and shouted robustly, gazing neither right nor left as if they were a single entity.

We children watched until they disappeared down the road, and we continued our own scraggly march.

"No talking," we were reminded as we went into the Commons.

First came the milk. I'd learned to drink it big gulps with several seconds' rest and normal breathing between gulps. Pleased to see pancakes with little tabs of butter instead of eggs, I prepared to tuck into the warm cakes set in front of me. Pancakes had always been my favorite breakfast food and I hadn't had any since I'd come to Synanon.

A dimpled girl I'd come to know as Deb asked me something I didn't hear.

"What?" I said.

"You," one of the demonstrators called out, pointing at me. "Leave. We said no talking."

I gripped the edge of the table.

My pancakes.

"What did I say?" The demonstrator lowered her hand and walked toward me.

"Please. I won't talk anymore. I want to eat."

"Up!"

"No." I sobbed, gripping the table harder. I couldn't believe this was happening.

Another demonstrator joined the first. They stood over me, arms crossed, waiting.

"I won't talk. I promise."

"You've lost the privilege. Get up. Now!"

My chest felt like it was closing with the mounting frustration that was bursting in gasps from my lips.

"I want to eat my pancakes," I whispered.

Their arms extended toward me.

As they pulled me from my chair, I grabbed two pancakes from my plate, shoving one into my mouth. The mounting pressure of frustration exploded from me in bits of doughy chunks that flew from my mouth.

"I want my pancakes! I want my pancakes!" I screamed, somewhat surprised at my loss of control over my temper. I refused to walk, so my feet dragged across the floor while the demonstrators pulled at my arms. One of them tried to pry my fingers from the crumpled pancake as I strained to get it to my mouth. I received a sharp slap across my face and was tossed out the sliding glass door to wait on the graveled road until breakfast ended.

Outside, there was no one. The sky, white with a blanket of cloud cover, stretched endlessly beyond the surrounding hills that engulfed the property. The dry yellow hills were empty and indifferent to my plight. Even nature appeared aloof, orderly and precise like the Synanon people the land sustained.

We didn't go to our usual classrooms after breakfast that day because, we were told, it was more important that as part of our back-to-basics lesson we children learn about environmental preservation. The lesson took place in the playroom in the form of a music class.

A man we'd never seen before sat on a chair in the middle of the room with a guitar in his hands. We were ushered in and guided to sit cross-legged on the floor around him. Then we waited while our demonstrator Keith stood off to the side, repeatedly smearing ChapStick over his lips. The tallest demonstrator and most reticent, Keith kept his communication with us children to the bare minimum of information.

In contrast, the man with the guitar seemed to speak volumes with his body alone. When he smiled, he flashed white even teeth and his brown eyes snapped and sparkled, reminding me of a golden retriever.

"Who here can tell me how we waste energy?" he said.

One of the boys raised his hand.

The man pointed to him.

"When we let the water in the sink run and we're not using it."

"What else?" the man asked.

"Leaving the lights on," a girl said softly.

"Yes. Yes. Whaddaya say we write a song about it? Who would like to write a song about the environment?"

Some of the kids, including me, perked up. Writing a song seemed like it might be fun.

The man strummed a few chords and hummed to himself. "Let's see, what should we say?"

"People all around wasting energy!" one of the kids yelled.

"That's good." The man hummed a little more to himself. After a few moments, his voice piped out, "Wake up! What do you see? People all around wasting energy."

The boy who'd suggested the line bounced on his knees, grinning.

"What else?" the man said.

Keith moved quietly for the door, applying more ChapStick. He exited the room just as several kids called out their ideas for the song.

In the end, we came up with:

Wake up! What do you see! People all around wasting energy.

Double it up, the temperature's down. Time to get up and turn it around.

Hey, hey, hey, how much have we saved today?

Hey, hey, hey, I know we're going to find a way.

I know we're going to find a way.

We sang the song over and over. A few hours later, we filed out of the room, remembering to keep silent on our walk back to the bunkhouses for our drill on hygiene.

Some of us girls were directed to the larger communal bathroom where we usually showered after physical education. Our group was greeted by a naked young woman. She instructed us to strip and step into the large shower stall.

We padded onto the damp tiled floor.

"Is everyone here?" she asked.

We turned our heads, looking around.

"Yes," a few of us replied.

"The two-minute shower," she said as if she were announcing the title of a book she was about to read aloud. "Watch carefully. First, you wet down."

She pulled up the metal shower handle, releasing a warm stream of water over herself and turning her body until she was completely wet. Then she snapped down the handle, shutting off the water. "Next, we soap." Grabbing a bar of soap, she lathered it between her palms, the suds bubbling and dripping down her slick wet legs and feet. Quickly, she ran the soap over her body, missing nothing. She lifted her large pendulous breasts, scrubbing the skin under them. She opened her thick muscular legs while her busy hand raked the soap over her vagina, pushing aside the folds to get into the smaller areas with a finger. Next the backside was attacked and last the head and face lathered. She set aside the soap, turned on the water and rinsed. "Two minutes. No more, no less. Your turn."

Under her scrutinizing gaze, we did as instructed. The demonstrated shower wasn't particularly different from the way we showered every day, yet we followed the instructions, keeping silent as we did.

Days went by and back-to-basics continued. When we children were not in a seminar or game, we listened to the adult games, broadcast, live or recorded, through radio speakers that were set up everywhere. Adults jogged up and down the roads, reinforcing exercise requirements that had been put in place a few years earlier.

Our calorie-restricted meals were a back-to-basics homage to the original "Fatathon" of communal weight loss, conceived as an incentive and encouragement for Chuck to follow his own doctor-ordered diet. It was much easier for him if the whole community became involved in his program, which was limited to a strict eight hundred calories a day. During the Fatathon blitz, there was tremendous pressure from the community for the overweight to shed pounds fast. Some members who were already lean grumbled about the mandatory health program. The complainers were verbally blasted into compliance, forced to winnow away pounds as well.

In back-to-basics, all of this came back, the diet requirements trickling down to the children in the form of toast without butter, meal portions cut sometimes by half and the abolishment of snacks.

Parents were told to stay away. We kids needed our space, management dictated. It mattered little to me because my mother was still in San Francisco.

On weekends our free time was confiscated for various projects. We were divided into small work groups. On my first job, I washed windows along with several other girls. We were given a bucket of mildly soapy water, a squeegee, roll of industrial paper towels and a short ladder. A demonstrator took us to the first bunkhouse and washed one of the windows for our benefit, wiping every smudge and streak away with the towel in the meticulous way that all chores were done.

We began on the first building, washing the windows inside and out. After an hour, my arms ached and my stomach grumbled from the hollow feeling of the calorie-restricted diet.

Julia and Rachel, who were on my team, had quit and were sitting on the gravelly pathway under one of the window ledges, chatting with each other.

For a moment, I stopped my work to look around. There were so many windows. It might take days to wash every window in every building.

Mary, the fourth member of our team, was up on the little ladder, her thin arm swiping at the glass over and over, her nose and cheeks red from the cold and exertion.

A group of boys passed us with a wheelbarrow of water repellent and wood preservative for the new jungle gym built recently in the play yard. A girl trailed behind them with a shovel.

"How long do you think it might take us to wash all these windows?" I asked Mary.

"How should I know," she snapped, glancing down. "Are you going to help me?"

"I've been working. What about them?" I pointed at the other two girls.

They both looked up, pausing in their conversation. Rachel said, "Mind your own business," but they both unfurled their skinny legs and stood up to resume the activity.

Minutes later, one of the demonstrators came to retrieve me. "Celena, come with me. I'm going to put you on socks with Chloe."

I followed the demonstrator to a vacant dorm building. We

climbed the porch steps and opened the door. Inside sat one small girl in a large room filled only with boxes. A formidable hill of mismatched socks lay in front of her next to an even smaller pile of matched socks tucked into each other. Off to the side were more socks of various colors and sizes laid out singly in long rows, all in need of a match. The box before her was half full of still more socks, but most worrisome were the boxes that had not yet been attended to. They filled the room in stacks.

Chloe glanced up at us, her narrow face wan with resignation and boredom, but her brown eyes lit up when she saw that she had company. We worked all day sorting, matching and talking.

The next day was a repeat of the first. I longed for the weekend to be over.

The following week our regular academic lessons were supplemented with more psychology, including a lesson about Freud's analysis of the human psyche and an introduction to Maslow and his theory of self-actualization. These lessons were over my head. Some of the older children understood the information, throwing out terms like "inner critic," "reality principle," "autonomy" and "transcendence" as we sat grouped at round tables, filling out charts and bubbles. Completely lost, I retreated into daydreams.

The next afternoon we were given a non-coed sex workshop. Having showered and changed into our pajamas, we were ushered into the living room to lounge on large throw pillows and beanbags, lending the feeling of a slumber party. Styrofoam cups of hot cider with cinnamon sticks were distributed.

Linda sat in a chair, waiting as we received our drinks.

Whisperers circulated among us about this newest seminar topic.

Once we'd settled down, Linda smiled, her round moon face gleaming in the subdued lighting. She spread her hands graciously, leaning toward us. "We are here to talk about our bodies and our sexuality. This is an open, safe space. You are free to say anything you like on the subject of sex and to share your thoughts." She sat back.

The silence provided its own sound, a ringing in my ears. Most of us were frozen with our cider in our hands. A few girls tittered.

Linda opened her hands magnanimously and I focused on her long slim fingers while I sipped my drink.

"At some point or another we discover masturbation, and it's a very nice feeling, wouldn't you all agree?" she said.

I swallowed the warm liquid in my mouth, but it went down wrong and I was sputtering.

"Who here masturbates?" Linda asked.

No hand went up. Even the giggling stopped.

"It's very natural," she said. "You don't have to be shy about it. Does everyone know what masturbation is?"

I squirmed on my pillow and glanced quickly about the room. Every face was red.

"How about you, Becky?"

At once, all eyes were on Becky. It seemed that even breathing stopped. Would Becky admit to this? The redness that flushed her face seemed to shoot up to the roots of her short blond hair. She shook her head vehemently, lowered her eyes and began to pluck frantically at the fringe of her pillow.

Please don't pick me, I prayed to myself.

"I mention masturbation," Linda said, "because for children it is the beginning of a healthy interest and relationship with our own sexuality, preparation for adulthood, when we begin having intercourse. Of course masturbation doesn't end in childhood. Adults masturbate, I masturbate, your parents do, everyone does, but usually no one likes to talk about it." She gave a little laugh. "I have even seen some of you girls masturbate when you didn't know I was looking. I won't name any names."

Torturously embarrassed, I wanted to be doing anything else at that moment—matching socks, washing windows, even watching the monumentally boring historical videos of ancient cultures that we were forced to look at as part of our curriculum—anything other than sitting in that room imagining my mother masturbating and Linda spying on us.

To our collective relief, Linda finally left the topic and moved on to the physical act of consummation between a man and woman.

A second demonstrator joined the lesson and gave us all the technical details of what happens during intercourse. "Sex feels really good," she gushed. "For women, though, the first few times can be painful because we have something inside of our vaginas called a hymen."

The sex lesson started in the afternoon and progressed into the night. Long, relentless and needling to our young minds, the lecture demanded our full attention.

At seven years old, I was not particularly interested in the smooth architecture of an erect penis or how many thrusts it might take for a man to ejaculate, although I was surprised to learn that it typically took between seventeen and twenty thrusts. When we took a break, I made a hole with one hand, then placed the index finger of my other hand into the hole with quick jabs, imagining the penis and counting. Somehow the total didn't seem right. The number seemed too few for something that was supposed to be so enjoyable.

We moved on to the subject of menstruation. A long, thick menstrual pad was passed around, complete with a slim white belt. I tried to understand that one day I would be bleeding out of my vagina and would need to wear the strange diaper-like thing. I felt dubious about this information and pondered it like I'd pondered the thrusting business.

Late that night, the workshop finally ended. We girls went to bed quietly, no doubt mentally numb from our strange seminar, exhausted from working and hungry from the diet.

"SNIP, SNIP," Chris said, cutting the air with his fingers. "All the men have vasectomies." He grinned sharply.

"What's a visectomy?" I asked, mispronouncing the word. We were shoveling loose dirt from a hole into a wheelbarrow. It was the weekend again, and I had been assigned to a team led by one of the men of the community. We were to dig long, narrow trenches for pipe installation.

"It's vasectomy, stupid. You know, it's something in the balls."

"What are you talking about?" I said. The image of a plastic container of tennis balls came to my mind.

"Balls." Chris raised his eyebrows and struck the earth forcefully with his shovel, grimacing while he pressed down on the blade with his foot for a deeper gouge. "Balls, the baby-making part."

I suddenly understood. Was this something that he had learned in the sex workshop we were all forced to attend? I did not remember hearing it, but maybe the vasectomy information was only for the boys.

"Their balls are cut off?" I asked.

"No, it's the part inside. It's just the men, though. You have to be eighteen." He grinned at me again, the kind of grin a boy gives when he's trying to be brave.

Although I later heard snatches of conversation between men and in the games on the Wire regarding vasectomies, I did not give it further thought. Later still, I learned the vasectomies were related to a program that also included forced abortions, another new word in my vocabulary. When I learned the meaning of the word "abortion," I felt some sadness, but again there was also indifference on my part. I found it hard enough trying to figure out my own predicament, let alone the opaque and bizarre world of the adults.

A year before I arrived to live in Synanon, Chuck Dederich had decided that he did not want any more children born into the commune; however, his analogy that childbirth was like a person crapping a football did little to quell the remorse and intense grief that women felt when they were forced to terminate pregnancies, some already advanced into midterm.

"We're not in the business of making babies here," Chuck said. "Fuck, we bring in children. There are too many goddamned children in this world."

That was Chuck's response to parents who begged for their unborn children's lives. In a speech, "Childbirth Unmasked: Teachings," Chuck ranted about the ills of having children and hoped to convince his members that birth was more ludicrous than miraculous. "Why does a woman want to have a baby?" he said. "Do you really know? Does a child mean value? Or is it just kind of a lark? Do you think there is any appreciable difference between a person who moves their bowels several times and those who do that once a day? Do you really and truly think that this natural process has any effect on the person doing it?

"I mean, what are you going to get out of the baby? Do you really want to go through an experience? I understand it's more like crapping a football than anything else. What do you want to do that for, for Christ's sake!

"The only reason we permit anyone to have children is to indulge the woman. This movement doesn't need children. We don't need it. We have millions of starving children, children who won't get education out on the streets. We have all the goddamn children we want. The only reason we have children is to indulge the woman.

"And one day we'll stop it. The problem is it's too expensive. All the motorcycles in Synanon together don't cost as much as to raise two children to the age of sixteen. All of them. When are we going to move ahead? When is it going to please everybody? I think the nuts had better realize we are going to move ahead now on this issue. Betty and I have been talking about this issue for damn near ten years. We're going to control birth like the wealthy people in the world have always done. The people who rule the world always control their births."

As part of the solution of Childbirth Unmasked, he decided that the men ought to do their part and avoid these kinds of travesties. They should get themselves snipped.

"The big slavery of women in modern life is that they're tied to that one child for eighteen years after the child is born," Chuck said. "Now the big thing that Synanon has done for women is to release them from that kind of bondage. The fact that they have residuals of longing to be back in that bondage doesn't mean that their release wasn't a good idea."

Makeshift clinics were erected as the Synanon doctors became very busy operating on the lines of men who arrived for their mandatory vasectomies.

Chuck never received the procedure.

"IF YOU WANT my body and you think I'm sexy, come on, sugar, let me know." Demonstrator Julie belted out the Rod Stewart song, rolling her enormous hips and stomach, which consisted of doughy folds of fat that obscured the crotch of her overalls. The dieting and jogging hadn't done much for her obese figure.

A few of us children stood idly in the play yard next to the Commons, watching. Her movements inevitably induced some giggles. Yet at any moment she could snap and get ugly with her words. I'd seen it before, but at the moment, humor crackled in her brown eyes, swallowed up by the fleshy sockets.

"Let me know, baby," she crooned seductively.

We exploded with laughter as she made kissing noises and winked at us.

Back-to-basics was winding down. Next week we would return to our regular schedule with our new and improved crew cuts.

CHAPTER SIXTEEN

God Does Not Exist

IT WAS the middle of the night, and I didn't feel good. For minutes, I lay on my side, not daring to move, knowing that whatever was making my stomach ache would come out of me if I attempted to sit up.

Lying still wasn't making me feel any better, though. Pushing myself up, I tried to jump from my bed, but the vomit spewed out onto my covers. Even when there seemed to be nothing left, my stomach muscles seized until I passed out from exhaustion.

Minutes later I awoke and, managing to get out of my bed, fumbled for my lamp, turning the switch on. My roommate slept soundly as I collapsed to my knees, vomiting again. Grayish chunks followed by red, runny liquid came out of me. It looked like blood.

I passed out again.

Minutes went by. My stomach seized. Frightened, I tried to

stand but felt too weak to get past my hands and knees. I crawled forward a little, then threw up a third time, thick, foamy red stuff. I wanted to wake my roommate, yet I was too weak to talk. I threw up six times that night and made it only to the door of my room before I finally fell into a deep sleep sprawled across the floor.

"Get up!" I opened my eyes to someone's sneakered foot nudging my arm. Morning had come. The demonstrator stared down at me, a look of supreme disgust on her face. "How dare you make a mess like this and not clean up after yourself?"

"I'm sick."

"What?"

"I'm sick," I managed to say a little louder.

"I don't care how you feel. You clean up all of this!"

My roommate appeared with a bucket of water and plunked it down next to me.

My stomach had eased somewhat while I'd slept, but as I pulled myself up, my head felt as light as a balloon. The room suddenly slanted. It seemed that every bit of strength I'd once possessed had been zapped out of me.

The demonstrator waited until I put my hand in the bucket to retrieve the soapy rag. "Clean up every last bit of this vomit and then shower and take yourself to class."

"I think I was bleeding inside," I said, trying to squeeze out the rag.

She turned on her heel. "I don't care."

The vomit had hardened into little hills, the blood having browned. I grabbed a chunk with the rag, pulled it off the carpet and deposited it into the water, my eyes warming with tears. I wanted my mother. I wanted to be hugged and loved. Even my aunt, who hadn't liked me, had let me rest when I was sick.

It took an hour for me to clean the throw-up from the carpet. Trembling to my feet, I carried the bucket to the bathroom, threw out the contents and washed the bucket until not a smudge of grime was left before I put it away in the utility closet.

After I showered, I felt a little better, but my stomach still felt hollow and sore. I walked alone to class, mentally pushing away the discomfort like I did during our mandatory runs when we were not allowed to stop and walk. It didn't matter if my side cramped or my legs ached. I'd learned to tolerate the aches and pains of running, and now I forced myself to tolerate the effects of the flu through a whole day of school and physical education. I needed to somehow forget that I was sick. It will go away, I told myself.

Months later a demonstrator took me to the little medical clinic on the property to cut out an earring embedded in my earlobe. I had not been able to remove the jewelry, so I'd left it in place and the skin had grown over it.

Taking notice of the odd lump in my earlobe, the demonstrator called me over and probed it, her brows knitted. "What is that?" she muttered to herself.

"My earring," I said.

"What?" She squeezed and pinched my lobe, her eyes squinted and lips compressed.

"I couldn't get it out," I said.

"Why didn't you ask for help?"

I shrugged, unable to articulate my lack of confidence in and distrust of the adults who cared for me.

Although I missed Theresa deeply, I saw her only rarely, as was dictated. When I did see her, I lapsed into baby talk, trying to regain what I had lost. When I babbled, she would laugh, then ask me why I talked like a two-year-old. I didn't know. I couldn't explain, so I would bury my face in her chest, trying to breathe in her scent of fresh soap and the natural, vanilla-like fragrance of her skin.

Once, when I visited her in her room, I asked, "Did you nurse me when I was a baby?" I knew the answer was yes, but I wanted to hear her affirm it.

"Yes, I nursed you until you were six months old."

"Can I try it?"

Theresa stood before me, her greenish eyes thoughtful. She sat on the edge of her bed and lifted her shirt to pull out her breast, still rounded and firm.

I took hesitant steps toward her until I could reach out my hand and touch her. I knelt down and placed my tongue to her nipple. She sat very still. I looked up and our eyes locked for a moment.

"Are you finished?" she asked.

I nodded, and she tucked her breast back into her bra.

When we didn't visit, we wrote to each other often. One piece of correspondence from her came in the form of a large heart cut from construction paper, with the words "I Love You" written in the center. When I read those words, I realized I did not want to live anymore. I did not want to be in Synanon. At my core, I felt abandoned.

Carefully, underneath, I wrote "Good by Momy I Am Died" and sent the red heart back to her.

When she questioned me about it later, embarrassment curdled my insides and I shrugged away from her scrutiny. So much time had elapsed that I'd moved beyond those feelings and further into my role as a Synanon kid. My earlier transgression seemed babyish and shamefully silly.

Just before my eighth birthday, Theresa received approval from upper management to move from the Synanon San Francisco house to the Walker Creek property where I lived. Management had taken advantage of her passion for wanting to participate in the school by giving her a job that nobody wanted with the promise that after a few years she could work her way into the role of demonstrator. The job involved the care of a physically and mentally disabled girl named Gwyn, who was afflicted with cerebral palsy. Because Theresa had questioned the lifestyle values of the school program, senior demonstrators wanted time to scrutinize her behavior. Her charge of Gwyn was a sort of probationary situation.

During a game, Theresa's suggestions that children spend more time with their parents and that parents be more involved in the school had settled in the VIPs' addled minds like

indigestion. They burped up their distaste in following games, spewing their disregard for her parenting philosophy. Her belief that children need to have a relationship with their parents was in direct conflict with Chuck's theory and experiment of creating distance and obliterating focused parental love, which he believed only weakened the individual. However, Theresa was not deterred from speaking her mind on this issue. Although she received a lot of flak for her "ridiculous and dangerous" ideas, she continued to stick to her unpopular opinion.

When Theresa could not be with me physically, she wrote; and when she visited, her visits were much longer than the usual parental visit. It seemed that every chance she had, she wanted to remind me that I was her daughter and that she deeply cared for me. Her love, when she could parcel it to me in the form of a quick kiss, wave or chat if we crossed paths, emotionally sustained me in the school's otherwise psychically erosive environment. I knew I was loved, and it helped me hold myself together.

Once Theresa and I were living on the same property, we began spending as much time together as we could. There were many weekends when she arranged for us to go on a picnic or have a sleepover.

Sleepovers were rare, but I enjoyed those times with my mother most of all because they reminded me of when it had been just the two of us and Synanon had not taken over our lives.

We'd have dinner, then go to Theresa's room, where we'd spend time looking over her record collection and reenacting her favorite musicals, coloring, cutting out paper dolls, reading storybooks and talking for hours. I discovered that Theresa could easily step into a child-like world and live there for hours, which created a kind of whimsy to our relationship.

"Did you know that if you stand very still and are really quiet, you might get a chance to see a fairy?" Theresa said to me one day while we walked through a small wooded area.

We stopped and looked up at the tops of the short trees that grew toward each other, creating canopies of branches that blocked out much of the sky.

"Shh," she whispered, eyes suddenly wide, index finger placed to her lips.

I watched her stoop down to peek behind some low plant growth, gently pushing aside a cluster of tall clover. Birds chirped and chattered around us. I knelt to have a look, too, my heart hammering in my chest, wondering whether she had found something.

Theresa was not pretending. The fairy world existed for her. When she spoke of the nature fairies to me, her green eyes would cloud over as if she were looking into that world.

"Let's sit down and wait," she suggested. "We have to let the little forest fairies know that they are safe with us."

We made ourselves comfortable on the earthy floor, neither talking nor moving for ten minutes or so. I remained attentive, alert to the movements of any shy elusive creatures that were only inches high.

Theresa finally gave a little laugh. "Come out, little fairies."

"Come out," I echoed.

When we saw not a single fairy, we finally stood and continued walking.

"Did you know, Celena, that there is a community in Scotland that gardens with the help of fairies?" she said.

"No," I said.

Theresa's eyes glowed. "It's simply amazing. All of the vegetables are triple in size." She raised her hands, opening them wide to show me how large some of the vegetables grew to be. "One day we'll have to visit. You won't believe it; it's just out of this world." She took my hand. "Would you like to see that one day?"

I nodded, and I wondered: *if we could go to Scotland, could we also go other places, like back to Los Angeles?*

"Theresa, do you think we'll always live here in Synanon?" I asked.

My mother's lips flickered in an attempt to keep her smile. "Synanon is a wonderful place in its own way. They have a lot to offer us."

We left the cloistered, wooded setting and walked back into the open.

I looked up at the curve of expansive blue sky and imagined the yawn of darkness beyond it. *What was beyond outer space? And where did the space come from? If, say, God put that space there, where did God come from?* My thoughts, mild at first, curled through my mind like wisps of smoke. *Where did God come from? Where did all the space come from? What if the space was always here? What if there was never a time when it wasn't? What if there is no time, if time doesn't exist?*

"Are you cold?" Theresa asked.

I was shuddering. I hated these types of thoughts. They snuck up on me sometimes, twisting my mind into a tunnel of confusion. How could something always have existed? I mentally pushed it all away and leaned into Theresa, forcing myself to think of the fairies.

"I DON'T THINK God is real," I said.

I'd been visiting with Theresa in her room, the two of us playing with paper dolls in a small corner by her record player. The bed took up much of the space.

Theresa glanced up at me from the cardboard figure of a smiling girl with shoulder length brown hair divided into two ponytails. She had been busy fixing a tiny wedge of green paper, a hat, to the girl's head, folding down the white tabs.

"God exists," she said, her slim eyebrows rising.

"I don't think so," I said.

"God is all around." Theresa waved her arms. "God is in us. God is nature." She pointed to a potted plant, then touched one of the new unfurling leaves. She was so sure of a greater celestial being.

Her comments furrowed into my young consciousness, trying to dislodge my skepticism, but it had already taken root. My Catholic education, hardly started and abruptly interrupted with my move to Synanon, faded in my mind like a drawing left out too long in the sun.

I did not have a close relationship with any of the demonstrators and as a result I had to sort out my own thoughts about the world around me, without guidance. Often I went around for months or years believing wrong conclusions about things. Trying to understand how radio worked, I thought live bands stood in line and took turns playing music. My ideas about the Bible were similarly haphazard. The Bible, I'd decided, must be a book of fairytales, but for grown-ups—stories written to interest adults, like *Grimms' Fairy Tales* for children.

Nobody in Synanon bothered with the Bible or Santa Claus, for that matter. Heaven, Adam and Eve, Santa Claus—all of it must be made up. The more I thought about what was beyond Earth, the more I felt that God had nothing to do with it. Possibly, God did not exist.

This idea troubled me. *If God didn't exist and God hadn't created the world, where did the world come from? The world had to have come from somewhere, but where? Space had to be something, but what?* I'd get choked up again. Sometimes it was hard for me to swallow, just thinking about it all.

"When I look up at the sky, I think, what's past the sky? There's space," I tried to explain. "How far does the space go? Where does it come from?" Waiting for an answer, I shot Theresa a look, but she didn't say anything. "What if there is just space, Theresa?"

Her expression appeared thoughtful. "Sometimes, in order to know God, we have to strike up a conversation with Him. You can tell God your thoughts. Maybe ask Him for a sign. He's good at giving signs."

"A sign?"

"Yes. A sign could be something that happens that has special meaning only for you. That would be God communicating with you. You could pray to God or write a letter; either way, if you really want proof, you'll get it."

Again, I noticed how sure of herself my mother seemed to be on this matter. She went back to dressing her paper doll.

In Synanon, at dinner, we would recite a prayer from St. Francis of Assisi:

Please let me first and always examine myself.
Let me be honest and truthful.
Let me seek and assume responsibility.
Let me understand rather than be understood.
Let me trust and have faith in myself and my fellow man.
Let me love rather than be loved.
Let me give rather than receive.

After that prayer, we would recite from Ralph Waldo Emerson's essay "Self-Reliance": *There is a time in every man's education when he arrives at the conviction that envy is ignorance; that imitation is suicide; that he must take himself for better, for worse, as his portion; that though the wide universe is full of good, no kernel of nourishing corn can come to him but through his toil bestowed on that plot of ground which is given to him to till. The power which resides in him is new in nature, and none but he knows what that is which he can do, nor does he know until he has tried.*

For the length of my time in Synanon, I would know these words by heart, but not their meaning. Chuck Dederich referred to Synanon as a religion, but other than the prayer at dinner, we didn't have any apparent rituals or religious ceremonies.

With the paper doll completely dressed, Theresa held it up for me to look at. "Isn't she cute? This is her traveling outfit. She's going on a long trip."

When I didn't respond, she set aside the cut-out paper girl and pulled me into her arms.

"God does exists, Celena. We'll talk about this later, okay? It's probably best not to talk about God to people here. They wouldn't understand."

CHAPTER SEVENTEEN

A Ban

WHEN MOST OF the toddlers from the Hatchery had outgrown their nursery environment, the demonstrators decided to move them to the Commons to have their meals and move the older children to eat in the Shed with the adults.

At my first meal in the Shed, I spotted Theresa fixing herself a plate of food at the buffet. I ran up to her to say hello and received a quick, bland smile in greeting.

"I'm not allowed to talk to you right now," she hissed before she walked to the adults' side of the room.

I wasn't sure what had just happened. My heart in my throat, I wanted to follow her and ask her to explain. A demonstrator told me to get my food and sit down. When I was slow to move, she barked the order again while walking toward me, adding, "You are spending too much time with Theresa. You need to focus on other things now."

I sat at one of the tables, my mind a scramble of panic. What did this mean?

The next day I ran into Theresa along the dirt road on the way to the Shed.

She looked over her shoulder and stopped for a moment.

"Theresa, why can't I talk to you?" I asked.

"We're on a ban from each other for spending too much time together. Soon it will be over, though." She started to say something more, but the same demonstrator who had yelled at me the day before suddenly emerged from the Shed. She watched us with her arms folded. Theresa dropped her gaze to the ground and continued on her way.

"It is a one-month ban," the demonstrator told me later. "You two are always walking arm and arm, hanging out with each other. That is not allowed here. Parents should not be with their children too much. Personally I find the behavior disgusting and Theresa a bad influence."

"But it's my birthday soon," I said.

"We are finished with this conversation, Celena. You can vent about it in the game."

Over the next weeks I saw Theresa now and then; however, she knew better than to even look at me and tried her best to ignore my existence. Perhaps she felt that the better she cooperated with the ban, the faster it might be over.

Instead, she spent all her time caring for Gwyn, who was a handful. The palsy had not rendered the girl immobile. She could walk with slow, jerky movements, dragging her right foot, which rolled at the ankle. Her arms curled in. Her speech was limited to grunts, chortles and screeches.

All of the children made fun of her, including me. We did not understand the challenges of her condition, and no one took the time to explain that although Gwyn had handicaps, she deserved dignity as well.

For the community, Gwyn was simply a burden, and Theresa, a misfit, was perfect for the job. I saw, though, that Theresa was tremendously kind to her and even seemed to believe that Gwyn had potential to improve beyond her present abilities. I often observed my mother patiently explaining things to her, someone I considered a pathetic figure. Gwyn would swivel her head, moaning and making what we children called "retarded sounds."

Along with the care of Gwyn, Theresa's other duties included washing the property's sheets and towels. We children were individually responsible for our own laundry, but the adults had a different system when it came to linens.

My eighth birthday came and went, yet Theresa and I remained banned from each other. Finally, after a month had passed, one of the demonstrators took pity on us and ended the forced separation. After that we were more careful about how much time we spent together.

The next time we visited, Theresa took me to my room and shut the door. "I have a present for you," she said. Into my hands she placed a thick book with a red cover and a picture of a gold chariot pulled by a team of white horses. "It is the *Bhaghavad Gita*. Open it to the middle, where there are pictures."

I flipped through the dense text until I reached the midsection, where I found enchanting images of exquisite beauty. I had never seen anything like it. Here were vibrant colors of blue, purple and pink, nature bursting in tuberoses, lilies and verdant green meadows. Cows were beautifully ornamented with necklaces of flowers, a smudge of red on their foreheads; they even wore earrings. Every picture also featured a magical, glowing, blue-skinned person with long dark hair and fine silk clothes.

"This woman is so pretty," I said.

"He is a man, and his name is Lord Krishna," Theresa said.

My gaze shot up from the book. I stared at my mom. Was she putting me on?

"This woman here is a man?" I pointed at the blue being to make absolutely sure we were talking about the same person.

"Yes. But he is a special man because he is actually an enlightened being. God sent him."

"Really?"

Theresa took the book and turned to a different page, showing me a picture of the blue man as a baby. She set the book back in my hands and said, "When Krishna was small, his mother found him putting dirt in his mouth. When she demanded he open his mouth, do you know what she saw?" Theresa's green eyes danced as she watched my face.

"What?" I asked.

"When he opened his mouth, she saw the whole universe. Can you imagine how shocked and surprised she must have been? That was when she realized that the universe is too much to understand."

Krishna's mother had glimpsed the visual of a concept that had been mentally plaguing me. I fell in love with the story, a great weight lifted off my shoulders. The epiphany of Krishna's mother became my own enlightenment in regard to my capabilities. I did not have to force myself to make sense of something far beyond my comprehension.

"Theresa, can I keep this book?" I asked.

"Yes. It's for you."

For weeks I carried the *Bhaghavad Gita* wherever I went and even slept with it, comforted by the pictures. Sometimes I tried to read the Hindu bible, but the ideas and philosophies expressed in the spiritual text were too complex for me to grasp.

In an attempt to spend time with Theresa while escaping the demonstrators' scrutiny, I took to hanging around the laundry room, helping her with the endless mounds of washing. Gwyn would be given a hand towel or washcloth to fold, and Theresa always made a big deal over the rumpled cloth when Gwyn was done "folding" it.

Whenever I wanted to be with Theresa, it seemed Gwyn was there, too, and I began to resent her. I thought of my mother and me as an already complete unit, like a hand with all five digits. Gwyn was an extra finger, dangling, useless and in the way. The other children found my association with the "retarded" girl as something more about which to tease me.

At mealtimes the demonstrators made allowances for me and other children to join Theresa and Gwyn at their table because Gwyn was technically part of the school. But watching Gwyn eat made me nauseated. She didn't close her mouth when she chewed, and I often got sprayed with her half-masticated food and saliva. Flecks of her dinner inevitably flew out of her open mouth when she sneezed, landing near my plate. At some point she would bite her tongue and yell in pain or purposely knock over a glass of milk, smirking when Theresa rushed to clean it up.

The specialness of having Theresa around began to wear off now that almost all of our interactions involved her needy charge. I stopped by the laundry room less often and chose to sit elsewhere at mealtimes when I could. A distance formed between us.

CHAPTER EIGHTEEN

Synanon Kid

"OOH, ahh. Yeah, baby. Do it to me," Melissa moaned as the voice of the Barbie doll she held.

Bending and twisting, she pried the doll's stiff rubbery legs apart. The short skirt, which barely covered the doll's crotch stretched up while the plastic hip joints strained in their sockets. Every time Melissa moaned for the doll, she contorted her own face into a strained grimace.

"There's a giant penis coming up out of the manhole," she said. "And it's fucking her. She likes it."

I stared down at the fuzz of carpet where the pretend manhole was supposed to be. It wasn't hard to imagine the manhole but I couldn't picture the penis. By then I had seen plenty of erections in the *Playboy*, *Penthouse* and *Hustler* magazines that some of the adults left lying around. Never, however, had I seen what would have been, in actuality, a three-foot-long penis.

"I don't think a man's thing is going to stretch that far," I said.

I reached under the doll and measured with my fingers. "His dick won't make it. She would have to squat down."

Melissa paused, frowning at me, her thick bushy eyebrows squeezing together almost into a unibrow.

"So," she declared. "It's pretend. He can have a giant penis."

"Won't her pussy be too small for a giant penis?" I said. "I don't think she would like it."

"Would you shut up? It's just a stupid fantasy. It doesn't have to make sense."

I shrugged, and Melissa returned to her moaning.

Melissa was several years older than me, and recently we had become friends. A tall girl with a strong lean build and vivid imagination, Melissa had the ability to gather a crowd by telling her own made-up stories or recounting the thrilling points of a book she'd read or movie she'd seen. She had only one parent in Synanon, her father, one of the commune's physicians.

Zissel, a Kibbutz kid from Israel who visited Synanon every year with her two brothers, reached out for the doll.

"Can I try?" Zissel's pupils dilated, eclipsing most of the normal brown of her eyes. Melissa's fantasy had excited her.

Just a few days before, Zissel and some of the other girls and I had been playing house. For almost ten minutes, Zissel and Janet disappeared under one of the blankets. Having grown increasingly curious, I finally lifted the blanket's edge to find the two of them tongue kissing, their bodies entwined.

Sex play was common, at least among us girls. We slipped into each other's beds at night and rubbed our bodies together, simulating the future sex we were told we'd be having one day. Just the same, this behavior wasn't cool. Girls often made out, then accused each other of being "a lesbo."

There was something thrilling yet icky about it all. Like the other girls, I was curious and turned on, but my feelings confused me.

I'd met another older girl, Michelle, in the back of a pickup truck, where we listened to Donna Summer's "On the Radio" while the driver did a run through the property and we helped with odds and ends. Michelle wore a knitted cap, the rim pulled low over her face. Her style seemed to fit the slick silky sound of Summer's voice as we sped through the dappled afternoon light.

For the first time I felt the angst of youth, that bubble of coolness where there is no room for adults. Michelle and I didn't move in the same circles, but after that truck ride I was aware of her noticing me. She had a strange habit of compulsively pulling out her eyelashes, several at a time. Her lids were bald from plucking. With no fringe of lashes, her dark eyes appeared hawkish.

"Hey, wait up."

I glanced over my shoulder to see Michelle jogging at a shuffling pace to catch up with me, her bald eyes squinting beneath the sun.

I stopped and waited.

"Where are you going?" she asked.

"Nowhere," I said. "To the dorms, I guess."

She took a few steps toward the shoulder of the road and the start of a narrow foot trail that led down to the creek bed.

"Come here," she said. "I want to show you something. Have you ever been down to the creek?"

"Yeah. Lots of times."

Michelle took my hand. "Come on. Come down there with me."

I let her pull me toward her, then I followed her along the path that snaked its way down to the water. When we reached the bottom of the trail, she stopped and looked back the way we had come.

I looked, too, wondering what she was searching for.

"Stand over here." She nudged me toward some thick foliage under the protective shade of brambly branches, the coniferous shadows darkening her eyes to black. Wordlessly she unbuttoned my pants.

I didn't try to stop her. It seemed I was not myself anymore. She pulled my pants down to my ankles. "Lie down," she ordered. I did as I was told, stretching out on the dry, pebbly earth.

Satisfied with my robotic obedience, she twisted her lips into a smile that never reached her black eyes. She removed her own pants and stepped over me, positioning the lower half of my body between her legs. For a moment she stood staring at me, then she sat, straddling me, her vagina resting against mine. She slowly rocked her hips, rubbing herself against me.

I couldn't feel anything, as if my sex had been anesthetized. The experience seemed to be happening to someone else, another girl lying there in the dirt, the real me an indifferent observer.

Faster she went until she was shuddering, pushing on my chest with her long thin fingers. She caught her breath, stood up and pulled on her pants. Without a word she walked back up the trail, leaving me lying on the ground with my pants twisted around my legs.

After that I did my best to avoid Michelle. If she caught me unawares and took my hand to lead me to some obscure place, I followed her without argument, numb, my mind gone blank. Mostly she pulled me into some forested area where she could feel me up, uttering the pornographic dialogue that ran through her head.

"This is what they do in *Hustler*," she'd whisper in my ear. "If you see any of those magazines, bring them to me."

I did as I was told, collecting what I found and handing the glossy books of smut over to her.

Other times she demanded I give her any of my possessions she fancied.

I had a hard time telling her no. When I'd pleased her, I basked in her praise. She'd tell me in her husky voice that I was her best friend and she would give the thing back to me later, but she never did.

I was enamored of her and hated her at the same time. It seemed that I could eventually be talked into anything that was self-deprecating. My personal boundaries were like a knee-high fence that anyone could step over.

"WE DARE YOU TO TRY IT."

I shook my head and shoved my hands into the pockets of my jeans.

"Oh, come on."

"No. I don't want to."

A group of us kids stood in a ditch by some scraggly bushes. Charlie, Carla and Amy huddled around a new boy called Daniel and me, with mean little smiles and squinty eyes. Just before they'd shown up, Daniel and I had been talking amicably. The three girls had whistled at us as they'd approached.

"Are you boyfriend and girlfriend?" Charlie called out.

I felt my skin grow warm as they closed in around us. I shot Daniel a look, but his face was as innocent and defenseless as a calf's. He hadn't been around these other children long enough to harden up.

"Leave us alone," I growled.

"Ooh! You want to be alone? Are you gonna kiss, kiss, kiss?" Charlie pushed her face into mine. Her smile was gone. The meanness traveled from her lips to her eyes.

"Shut up," I hissed. "Fucking bitch."

She pulled her face back and the smile returned. "I'll give you something if you both pull down your pants and let your things touch."

Daniel's cheeks blazed, and I felt sorry for him. Although he and I were both eight, he seemed much younger than the rest of us.

I also knew he was embarrassed about a previous incident: when we'd been naked in the shower, he had asked me if he could give me a hug. I had said no. Why we'd been showering together will forever remain a mystery to me.

The other two girls had grown quiet.

"No," I repeated. I felt trapped.

"Carla, show her your markers," Charlie said.

Carla looked doubtful as she held out the plastic book of Pentel markers. I took the book and snapped it open, staring at the extensive array of colors. They were dazzling. One of my favorite hobbies was drawing girls and coloring them, or I would make a loopy, scribbled mess with a pencil, then color all the parts with different shades. It would be nice to have some Pentels. I only had access to crayons.

The girls waited.

Daniel said, "I'll do it."

I handed the package of pens back to Carla. "Nah. I don't think so."

"We won't tell," Charlie said in a hushed voice. "We'll make it a blood secret."

I didn't want to do what they'd asked, yet I found myself saying, "You won't tell? And I can have the pens?"

"Yeah. I swear," Charlie said.

She dug into her overalls pocket, pulled out a pocketknife and opened the small blade. We all watched as she made a thin slice across the pad of her index finger and a drop of blood welled up to the surface. Carla held out her finger. Charlie cut each of us, then we meshed our bloody fingers against one another's to seal the deal.

"Okay," I said. "Give me the markers."

"You've got to do it first, then we'll give them to you," Charlie said.

Daniel unbuckled his pants and pushed them off his hips.

I unbuttoned my jeans. Our pants sagged around our hips while the girls watched, eyes wide.

Daniel stepped up to me and pushed his pale hips in my direction, his tiny, limp penis nudging against my vagina.

I looked at the girls. Charlie held her hand over mouth, then removed it to shriek, "Oh my God, that is so disgusting!" A wave of shame washed over me. I grabbed my pants, yanking them up as the girls started to run away.

"Hey!" I screamed, trying to button and move at the same time.

Their laughter echoed at me.

I grabbed a stone and threw it in their direction, but it fell to the ground a few feet away.

They were gone.

"Shit!" I said.

"I'm sorry," Daniel said. He shoved his shirt into his pants, his light brown eyes soft with an affection that I couldn't understand. My chest was tight with anger that threatened to turn to tears.

"Stay away from me," I hissed.

In that instant I could see that he knew that we were not friends and never would be. He ducked his head and walked away while I remained rooted, hyperventilating.

Over the course of just one year in Synanon, between the ages of six and seven, it seemed I had lived a lifetime. The little girl who wore pigtails and short skirts and attended etiquette school and learned to say, "If you please, ma'am," followed with a gracious curtsy, was no more.

In her place was someone I doubted that any of my family would recognize. I strutted about in my blue jeans, white t-shirt and cowboy boots, my speech quick and peppered with the f-word.

Anyone in Synanon who didn't learn to talk fast and take up space was verbally run over by others. In the game there was usually a point when everyone turned on one person. You had to know how to take it and not crumble when ten, fifteen or twenty people all screamed at you, telling you what a fucker you were, a complete shithead, not worth two cents. The gamers would lean forward in their chairs, eyes wide, neck veins popping, fingers pointing as if invisible leashes held them from springing forward to devour the person in the hot seat. The rule was that you must stay in your chair.

"I'm going to tear you apart! You're gonna wish you were dead!" they'd yell.

"You think anyone here likes you? Who here likes Celena? No one! We hate you! Hate you!"

Throughout my years in the commune I had nightmares about being attacked by a bear or wolf. I was trapped in a circle of children, all of them mouthless and holding hands. Only I was confronted by a wild animal. The other children either would not or could not help nor let me get free of the beast that crept ever closer with its sharp fangs.

When I first came to the school my popularity among my peers burned brightly, bolstered by my second buddy Anna, who had taken Sophie's place. Socially, Anna was at the top and anyone she deemed worthy of her company basked likewise in the warming rays of her alpha status.

When Anna left a few months into my stay, my popularity dropped like a rapidly declining currency. Girls who'd previously included me began to turn their backs, teasing me mercilessly, imitating the way I walked on my toes. The shape of my head was mocked, the long narrow proportions of the back of my skull like the profile of Nefertiti. This inspired the nickname "Football Head."

I didn't know how to handle such cruelty. One day I would react with tears, another with rage. There were times when I played nicely with a particular child for several days or weeks only to have him or her suddenly turn on me or join a small mob of children who would taunt me to the point of verbal savagery.

I knew the game forbade physical contact, but outside of the game I frequently had physical fights with the other children. One of these fights led me to take up a new activity.

Every week I looked forward to the show *Little House on the Prairie*. During that hour I soaked up the love that Ma and Pa had for their children, virtually living the frontier life. I'd go to the shared living room in my pajamas, ready for another riveting hour of Laura Ingalls's life, her chores at home with Ma, lessons in the little school house, experience with the great outdoors and always at the heart of it, a moral lesson to learn that Pa would usually drive home in his calm and kind way.

I was therefore severely disappointed when one evening a cop show with a car chase and people shooting at one another was on the TV instead of *Little House*. Most of the kids hadn't come to the living room to settle in yet. Just three boys sat in front of the TV.

I asked, "What happened to *Little House*?"

One of the boys, Ben, glanced up blandly at me. "We're not watching that tonight. Everyone wants to watch *Kojak*."

"We always watch *Little House*." I felt my frustration rising. I had waited a week for my favorite show and now faced the chance of not getting to see it because of dumb *Kojak*.

"Well, we're watching this," Ben said, his attention focused on the TV.

Who put him in charge? I marched up to the TV and changed the channel.

Ben jumped to his feet and ripped my fingers from the dial.

"Hey! We were looking at that!" he screamed in my ear.

"This is not the show we're supposed to watch!" I screamed, my retort earning me a solid push.

It was all I needed to completely lose my temper. I sprang on Ben and grabbed a handful of his cheek, yanking as hard as I could. I did not see his fist, but in the next instant it had connected with my nose. I don't remember the pain, only the surprise and fear from the blood that spurted out.

"Put your head back," Ben instructed.

The fight was clearly over as the other two boys, Mike and Eric, jumped to their feet to get a glimpse.

Too hysterical to follow any instruction, I wailed.

"Put your head back," Ben yelled as I watched blood drip from my nose onto my shirt. Reaching out to grab my shoulder, he steadied me and gently lifted my chin. "Keep it back like that," Mike advised, hovering over me next to Ben. "It'll stop the bleeding."

"I'll get some toilet paper," Eric said. A minute later he was back with a small wad, which I placed over my face, pressing it against my nose. I slowly brought my head to neutral while the boys watched.

The bleeding had stopped.

Mike grinned. "Did you see the way she jumped you?"

Ben laughed, then we were all laughing and reliving the fight.

"You're strong for a girl," Ben said. "You should come box with us."

He slapped me on the back, and Mike did as well.

My pajama top was spattered with blood. I went to my room to change it, and when I came back, more kids had come into the living room to watch TV. *Little House* was on, and Ben gave me a quick grin as I settled in with the group.

A few days later I joined some of the boys in their dorm for boxing lessons from our physical education teacher, Buddy. While we waited for him, we arm wrestled one another, and I beat most of my opponents.

Buddy arrived, carrying two sets of boxing gloves. He had us form a ring around the fighters. We were already warm and a little sweaty from arm wrestling, and the small room soon filled with our musky body odors. The fighters went at it while the rest of us yelled and cheered. The fight lasted only a few minutes, but I was wildly excited. When Buddy asked who wanted to fight the winner, my arm shot up. A roar of cheers erupted from the boys, their faces glistening with moisture. Some grinned so widely it seemed their skin might split.

I stepped into the ring and the referee laced my gloves. I did not know the rules of boxing, and no one bothered to explain them.

When Buddy rang the little bell, I rushed my opponent and lifted the surprised boy off his feet. The room exploded with shouts as I swung him around amid his angry cries of "Put me down!"

For the finale, I threw him, but as we were the same size, we both went flying. My contender landed on his hands and knees with me on his back. Dazed, he sagged through his midsection as the referee jumped in for the countdown.

When my opponent didn't get up, the ref grabbed my arm and announced me the winner.

The boy, finally catching his breath, jumped up, yelling, "That's not how the game goes!" His words were drowned out by the other boys' yells that he'd been "beat by a girl."

I continued to box with the group for several weeks until the lessons faded like many other activities in the community.

Without that outlet, I began to have rages. The first came over me one afternoon when I was relaxing in my shared room and listening to Shawn Cassidy's "Da Do Run Run" blaring from Charlie's record player.

During one of our many moves, I wound up sharing a room with my enemy and two other girls. Our four twin beds were angled to give the most privacy possible, but it was still a tight fit. We were all in the room that day, languid and lazy, each sprawled on our own bed and absorbed in a personal activity.

I flipped through a picture book as Charlie began to sing along with Shawn Cassidy. Small for her age, Charlie had sleek, dark looks and a natural propensity toward horses and Nancy Drew novels. Part of the popular clique, she never let me forget that she considered herself far above me in social ranking. Her glares, sneers and eye rolls indicated her feelings.

"The doody run run run. The doody run," Charlie belted in her young, high voice.

The other girls giggled and so did I. I wasn't as big a Shawn Cassidy fan as some of the other kids were. With his feathered hair, red lips, cutesy puppy-dog look and silver disco jacket, he was too effeminate for my liking.

"Yeah, Celena shit in her pants. Yeah, she's a stupid bitch. The doody run run. The doody run," Charlie sang.

Laughter exploded from the other girls, and I felt my throat close as I tried to focus on my book. My eyes were watering, but something other than sadness was building within me.

"Yeah, Celena stinks so bad," the other girls joined in, singing at the top of their voices.

I threw down my book, sprang from my bed and marched over to Charlie. When she saw me approach, she sputtered with laughter. I grabbed the needle of her record player and dragged it back and forth across the album. The loud screeching sounds rendered an instantaneous halt to the humor.

"Hey! What the fuck are you doing?" Charlie jumped up, but my hand shot out, hitting hard against her small chest. She fell back, worry flitting across her dark eyes. I wanted to destroy her and everything else. I pulled the album off the player and threw it across the room. A static quiet took the place of the cheerful pop beat as my roommates gazed at me, stilled from shock.

I grabbed Charlie's lamp, tore it from the outlet and threw it with such force that it smashed against the wall.

"Stop that!" one of the girls said.

The fear in her voice only fueled my anger. I turned on her, but she scrambled away, so I grabbed her bed covers, stripping the mattress and pulling it from the box frame. My strength turned Herculean. I threw more lamps and overturned nightstands. Guttural sounds tore from my throat.

"Celena, stop it! Stop it!" Charlie yelled. "We're sorry!"

I ran from the room and out into the sunny afternoon. Under a tree lay Sophie, curled on a blanket and reading. I hated her. I hated that we were always thrown together. In my fit, I grabbed the top of her book, but she held tight, staring at me, her eyes begging me to leave her alone. "What are you doing?" she whined. "Stop it."

I pulled harder at the book, dragging her along the ground until she screamed. Then I ripped the book from her fingers.

"Please! Don't do that!" she cried.

I tore out the pages, flung the book aside and jumped on her, hitting her over and over. When she covered her head with her arms and curled to protect herself, I kicked at her hands, until someone grabbed and restrained me.

Several seconds passed while a demonstrator roughly shook my body, shaking me out of the blackness. I heard sobbing. It was Sophie, curled like a pill bug, her fingers already swelling.

I'd wanted to kill her.

CHAPTER NINETEEN

Hit and Run

SOMETIME AFTER THAT another child was hurt much more severely.

We were on a field trip, clustered near a building that might have been a store, somewhere along a road. The Synanon school bus waited at the top of a steep driveway. Two of the boys and I separated from the group and ran down the driveway to the curving highway, which was flanked by redwood trees. One of the boys, Brett, and I decided to cross, but I changed my mind and went back to the shoulder. I was crossing; then I wasn't. Somehow I knew to stay back even before I saw the car.

I may have yelled for Brett not to cross; or maybe I didn't. I do not remember.

A car shot out from around the curve of the highway. A giant wave of metal swept Brett off his feet. His body flipped onto the hood, bounced high into the air, then fell to the pavement. A tennis shoe landed at my feet.

The car kept moving. Inside it, black-haired children with large, dark, round eyes screamed against the unfolding nightmare. As if the driver were on a mission to kill my friend, the car slowed, pushing Brett's body down the highway. In the passenger seat, a woman clutched at the driver's arm while he remained bent over the steering wheel.

One moment I was at the side of the road; the next I was up the driveway by the building, but behind a chain-linked fence.

The car pulled over and children poured out. The woman clutched a red-faced baby, all mouth, its cries shrill and loud. She and the man talked over each other in Spanish.

Brett lay abandoned, curled up on the road, slowly, noiselessly opening his mouth like a fish on dry land. His body convulsed with one big shudder, then he was still.

It seemed the occupants of the car were on the run. From what I didn't know. Later I discovered that the driver had stolen the car. He had five children of his own, but if not for his wife, he wouldn't have pulled over.

Brett was not killed. He remained alive, but in a comatose state for quite a while. After he was released from the hospital, he returned to the Synanon school, where he became the business of the demonstrators.

We were told that we could look at Brett, but we needed to keep quiet in his room. One by one, we stepped up to the large crib where he slept like a giant toddler and peered at his still form.

He slept for days. Once in a while he opened his vacant brown eyes and looked around. Everything he'd learned throughout the eight years of his life, his personal experiences, which made him uniquely Brett had all been wiped from his mind. He did not even know his name.

Gradually he stayed awake for longer periods, but didn't talk. He'd become an infant again. He didn't understand anything. We talked to him like he was a newborn. Sometimes he would smile.

After some weeks he began to speak, but only one word at a time. Most communication consisted of reminding him of the word or name for each and every thing. He would point at objects, and we would tell him, "That's a sock." "That's paper." "Those are flowers." "Yes, that's your nose."

Within a month, he recovered a slow, stuttering form of speech accompanied by rapid blinking. Later he became strong enough to use a wheelchair. A few months after that he graduated to crutches and his words were interrupted less frequently by the stutter.

A year after the accident, Brett walked and ran about like normal. The only indicators of his having been mowed over by a speeding car were two long scars along his outer thighs from hip to knee and an occasional sticking of words he would repeat five or six times like a scratched record.

CHAPTER TWENTY

A Visit With My Father

"GUESS WHAT?"

I'd been lying in bed ready to go to sleep when Theresa poked her head into my room, her eyes shiny and happy as she beamed a smile at me.

Surprised to see her during non-visiting hours on a school night, I sat up and rubbed my eyes while she made herself comfortable at the foot of my bed.

"What are you doing here?" I asked.

She covered my hand with hers and made a quiet little squeal. "I'm getting love matched."

"I thought you were love matched to Larry."

She waved her hand as if she were pushing Larry into a cosmic waste bin. "That didn't work out. He wasn't the one. But, oh, Celena, my new husband is going to be Andrew. He's so wonderful! I can't wait for you to meet him. And he's really funny; he used to be an actor. He's the one who sometimes wears the gorilla outfit."

I was intrigued.

From time to time a man showed up at the school dressed in the furry costume. He would walk around like an ape, hold out his ape hands for the kids to slap him five and basically make an ass of himself. I never found him particularly funny, though a lot of other people did. As I tried to reconcile the images of her and a gorilla man, my mother talked.

"He is going to be your new dad," she said.

A new father.

But *where* was my dad? Did he know where I was? A faint echo pushed through the morass of amnesia. Would I ever see my father again? A familiar heaviness settled in my chest, and when the first warm tears slipped down my cheeks, Theresa, now just a blurry image, asked me what was wrong. She stroked my forehead.

"I miss my dad," I said under my breath. It felt hard to talk.

"You miss your dad?"

I nodded and wiped at my eyes.

She looked away for a long minute. "You know what? I'm going to arrange for you to have a visit with him."

"You can do that?"

"I promise." She smiled and kissed me. When her gaze held mine for a moment, her eyes told me it was all settled. "I should go," she said. "I've already stayed too long."

We hugged each other, and she left after wishing my roommates a good night.

A few weeks later I boarded a van with Theresa to spend a weekend with her and her new husband, Andrew, at the Marin Bay property. Children rarely set foot on the Bay property, which was reserved mostly for VIPs' homes.

On the first night of my visit Theresa and I met Andrew in

the dining hall for gracious dining, Synanon's version of a gourmet restaurant.

When I first glimpsed Andrew's face without the gorilla costume, I was surprised to discover he was magnificently ugly. For the first few minutes I couldn't stop looking at him. His eyes seemed too close together under his prominent forehead. His lips were big for a white man's, his nose shaped somewhat like that of a pug's. He had the figure of a boxer and wore slacks and a buttoned-up long-sleeve shirt.

A smile danced at the corner of his lips, and anything he said sent Theresa into a fit of giggles. Her flushed cheeks and shiny eyes enhanced her natural beauty.

Having learned the word "sexy," I saw that that was how Theresa saw Andrew. Were there ways to be sexy that I didn't know about? I waited for a natural break in the conversation, then asked, "Excuse me, but are you a sexy man?"

My question broke through the giggles and harrumphs and landed in an awkward silence followed by a bellow of laughter. "Honey," Andrew said to me in a booming voice, "I'm so sexy I can't stand it."

"Oh," I said.

His answer disappointed me. I'd hoped he'd say no and thought that I'd somehow misunderstood something along the way.

During dinner I fired off a litany of off-color penis and potty jokes that we children found hilarious. Having spent so little time in the company of adults, I was out of touch regarding appropriate, respectful dialogue between a child and her elders.

"Did you hear the joke about these three men, a white guy, a black guy and a Chinese guy?" I said.

"No." Andrew smiled and leaned his elbows on the table, resting his face in his palms.

"Well, there were three men: a Chinese, a white and a black

trying to talk the devil out of sending them to hell," I said. "The devil said, 'If you want the chance of not going to hell, let me hold your dick and if it doesn't melt, you can go to heaven.' They all wanted a chance to not get thrown in hell. The Chinese guy went first. His dick melted, so he went to hell. Next came the white guy. The same thing happened to him. Finally, it was the black guy's turn. When the devil held his dick, he was surprised because it didn't melt." I paused to give the punch line maximum effect. "The devil asked him, 'How come your dick didn't melt?' And the black guy said, 'It melts in your mouth, not in your hands!'"

Andrew stared at me, blank-faced.

"Do you get it? It's like the M&Ms commercial. Melts in your mouth, not in your hands," I sang.

Andrew still didn't laugh. Maybe he hadn't seen that commercial, I thought, so I tried another joke, an easy one about a person staying in a hotel room who hears small voices moaning from the bathroom.

"'When the log rolls over, we're all going to die!'" I said, imitating the voices. "The person freaks out, grabs his stuff and checks out of the hotel. Then another person checks into the room. He hears the voices, freaks out and runs out of the room. Then a third person checks into the room. He hears the voices and is curious, not scared like the others, so he enters the bathroom to check things out. He looks careful-like into the toilet bowl and guess what he finds? A group of ants sitting on a turd."

I laughed myself silly at this punch line, but Andrew didn't seem to get the joke.

"All right," I said. "This one's really funny." I was about to launch into the joke about a man who was supposed to gather golf balls, but tried to get King Kong's balls instead, when Andrew leaned toward Theresa and whispered into her ear. Her cheeks tinged with red, she stood up and motioned to me to follow her. We went out to the foyer.

"Celena, Andrew wants you stop telling the penis jokes and poop jokes. They're making him uncomfortable."

I felt my face grow hot. I thought I was being such a great dinner partner. We returned to the table, and for the rest of the meal I barely looked at Andrew.

THERESA MADE good on her promise and a trip was arranged for us to go to Los Angeles to visit my father and other relatives for a weekend. Later she told me that she hadn't requested the visit outright, predicting that the request would be turned down. Instead, she'd applied for welfare, knowing Synanon would gladly accept the money. She then told management that since the organization was receiving public aid, my father had a legal right to visitation.

We arrived at my grandparents' home in the early evening. It felt strange to be back at the house where I'd spent my days in refuge from Aunt Terry, who lived across the street. My father arrived shortly after we did, seeming to burst through the door.

"Hey!" he called.

"Daddy!" I ran into his open arms, and he held me tight, laughing, his voice deep and rumbling. His warmth seemed to spread into my own being. He smelled of aftershave and spicy cologne. His shiny brown face and large forehead gleamed in the light. His dark eyes crackled with humor. I felt as if we had seen each other only yesterday.

My father sat on the sofa and pulled me onto his lap. "So how have you been, sweetheart?"

For a moment I didn't know where to begin, but before long we were deep in conversation, other relatives joining in to ask me about Synanon and what it was like to live there.

"My, you're getting to be a big girl," my father said, patting my legs. "Your grandma used to tell me when you were four years old, 'Jim that girl is too old to be sitting on your lap.' And I told her, 'Mama, she'll never be too old. She'll be forty, and I'll still have her sit on my lap.'"

My uncles threw back their heads and laughed with my father, and I nuzzled my face against his neck. I could see Grandma Regina laying plates on the kitchen table, a small smile on her lips.

As usual she busied herself in the kitchen with the feast she'd prepared. There was gumbo made with shrimp, sausage and chicken, rice, corn bread, green beans julienne, bread pudding, pies, soda and coffee.

My cousins and Uncle Joe came over from across the street, but Aunt Terry did not. "Our mom said to say hi," they told me. "She's not feeling well." The mention of her name had a slightly souring effect on my mood; however, I felt too excited to be with my family and father to give her much thought.

After dinner I cuddled next to my dad, resting my head against his chest so I could hear the resonant base tones of his voice. The combined laughter of my uncles was thunderous, an earthquake of sound that vibrated off and through the walls.

A few hours into the visit, my cousins wanted me to go across the street with them to their house. I went. Nothing had changed. My gaze swept the same worn furniture and brown carpet. The air held the stale smoke of cigarettes, a signature smell. Fear tickled my skin as I recalled my younger self, an apparition encapsulated in a time past. When I glanced toward the kitchen, the image of my small body being dragged across the linoleum, the angry blows of plastic racetracks ripping into my skin, clouded my memory.

My cousins, unaware of or unwilling to acknowledge my discomfort, pulled me toward their bedroom. In the hallway I glanced over my shoulder at the room opposite theirs. A shroud of sorrow emanated from the static of the closed bedroom door. I knew my Aunt Terry was in there. *Hiding?* I wondered.

Giggling, my cousins led me into their own room, flopping on their beds to stare, amazed, at the drastic change in my appearance. They plied me with questions. What was it like to be almost bald? To live in a place like Synanon?

I answered, reveling in the attention.

My visit lasted an evening and ended all too soon.

I would not see my father again for two years.

CHAPTER TWENTY-ONE

Girls and Bald Heads

I HEARD SOMEONE CRYING.

The soft sounds of sniffling seemed to come from the bathroom. The door stood open a crack, and I poked my head in. One of the girls who lived in my dorm, Carol, stood glaring at her reflection in the mirror. Her bloodshot eyes were slits in the puffy wet skin that surrounded them. The tips of her ears were flaming red. In the dim lighting, her recently shaved scalp gleamed pale. Her face, swollen from crying, had lost any male or female characteristics. She appeared inhuman.

The movement of my image in the glass pulled her from her trance. She spun around, lunging for the door as I tried to close it.

I wasn't fast enough.

Her hands grabbed at my face, her nails slicing long rakes in my cheeks while she shrieked her fury. Then, just like that, she was back in the bathroom, slamming the door after herself.

My face felt like it was on fire. I covered my cheeks with my hands just as two girls came down the hallway and darted past me into one of the bedrooms. "Get in the closet," one of them hissed.

A demonstrator soon followed. When she spotted me, she caught hold of my shoulder, marching me in front of her and out of the bunkhouse to the deserted courtyard. Minutes before there had been groups of kids everywhere, but they'd dispersed like roaches exposed to the sudden glare of light. I heard whispering and saw a face or two pressed against a window as I was marched toward the playroom. I didn't try to fight or run away. The head-shaving was going to happen. It was better to not make a fuss.

In the playroom several chairs were lined up, each with a demonstrator standing behind it. In their hands were electric clippers. I sat quietly, though my stomach felt like a cage of fluttering winged insects.

The ceremony was interrupted by high-pitched screams and sounds of struggling. Donna and Carlene had been caught. They were both part of the popular crowd, with their stylish Wrangler jeans and halter-tops they'd bought with their allowance. In their record collections, they had the cool albums like *Saturday Night Fever* and Abba's *Dancing Queen*. They even smelled cool, like Hubba Bubba bubble gum and Dr. Pepper-flavored Lip Smackers.

Carlene's blond hair had grown into soft curls around her ears, giving her a more feminine look compared with the spikes she sported when her straight hair was only a few inches long. Donna's thick beaver pelt had grown into a pageboy look, which she was able to feather in the front.

They flung back their lithe bodies, digging in their heels. Waiting demonstrators ran to help their colleagues, wrestling the girls toward the chairs. Carlene's small body buckled into the seat, the chair almost flying backward from her spasmodic motions.

Donna was going for the face as Carol had. With her fingers curled like claws, she charged one of the demonstrators. The woman jumped back just in time and the distraction was sufficient to allow someone else to grab Donna and secure her with a silky cloth rope that was wrapped around her upper body, pinning her arms at her sides.

"Look at Celena and how quietly she sits," one of the demonstrators said.

"Fuck her! Fuck you!" Donna yelled. Her face filled with blood, seeming as if it might burst as a demonstrator held her head still against her will. Carlene had given up, breaking into sobs. Watery mucus dripped from her nose.

The buzz of the clippers rang, and I felt the comb vibrate over my scalp as chunks of hair fell onto our shoulders and laps. It took only a few minutes to have our hair shaved to a quarter of an inch.

The demonstrators passed around oval hand mirrors, seemingly oblivious to our distress. This was "act as if" at its finest.

"Take a look at how beautiful you are now," a demonstrator said to me.

I couldn't stomach looking in the mirror. I avoided mirrors whenever I could. I already knew how I looked: a narrow skinny head with big, dark, haunted eyes.

In my dresser drawer was a knitted hat I'd tucked away for these occasions. Every moment that I was allowed I would wear that hat until my hair grew back to some semblance of normalcy. For days we girls skulked around, startlingly odd-looking with our newly shaven appearances until time wore away our timidity and awkwardness and we were once again ourselves.

A few days after the mandatory haircuts, a group of us girls were rounded up again.

"Come, come!" two of the demonstrators beckoned.

The summons was for a special tea party at the Big House. A large, white, plantation-style home on the property where Chuck and Betty had once lived was now a museum of sorts. I was given a shiny, poufy dress the color of pale pink frosting, which clashed with my dark skin and reddish undertones. The fabric, stiff and unyielding, caged my boyish muscular body and long neck. I was freakishly eye-catching wearing this princess attire while sporting my newly shaven look..

I joined my peers on the dirt road, each bedecked in her own spectacular atrocity. We followed the demonstrators, who were also queerly dressed, with their cheeks carefully rouged and eyes enveloped in giant, spidery, fake eyelashes.

We walked up a hill to the plantation home, climbed up to the wide porch and went into the main parlor, where we were led to small round tables dressed in gossamer white tablecloths and set with fine china.

We sat, stuffed into our chairs, sipping tea from delicate, rosebud-decorated cups while we listened in resignation to talk about our status as the daughters of Synanon: beautiful girls with lovely bald heads and healthy bodies. After tea we were made to walk back and forth across the room with our heads held high. Each of us was guided to a full-length mirror, where we were instructed to gaze upon our "extraordinary beauty."

After two excruciating hours we finally said goodbye to our hosts. When we filed out of the building, the sun sat low in the sky. "Wait, wait," the demonstrators called, gathering together our rapidly dispersing group. "We're going to take a group picture before you return to the dorms."

Huddled with my peers before the majestic facade of the Big House, I squinted into the light of the setting sun, focusing on the hills that hugged the property. Orange and gold spilled across the great expanse of earth, setting the long dry grass afire with liquid color melting into darkness.

    A cold breeze ruffled my dress..

    "Smile! You are Synanon girls!"

    Hearing the click of the camera, I closed my eyes.

CHAPTER TWENTY-TWO

Wildlife

I SLAPPED the cow's backside, her bony shanks rising up from her deep sway back.

Her head swung around and she gave a low moan, pushing air through her large nostrils as she turned in my direction.

She was too slow.

I'd already jumped out of her reach, laughing and dancing before her.

She charged toward me, her groaning moo more angry. She'd taken only several steps when one of the boys ran up behind her, slapping her rump. This brought her to a halt and then a change of direction as, disoriented, she ran toward no one.

We howled with laughter, calling out to get the cow's attention. She was an older, dimwitted animal that sometimes wandered through the courtyard of our dormitory buildings. Often she was slow-moving, but sometimes she broke into a hot rage and began charging us. We'd dash to one side then the other as she swung her neck, mooing and running a few steps here, a few steps there. We'd tease her until the demonstrators caught sight of us and put a stop to this cruel activity, shooing us inside.

One day the mad cow disappeared. Perhaps she was put down for our safety.

A large variety of creatures lived on the Walker Creek property: horses, cattle, sheep, pigs and a small zoo composed of rabbits and chickens, which we were allowed to keep as pets. There were two blue heelers, Bob and Jody. They were often engaged in activities required of working ranch dogs, such as rounding up sheep and cattle.

There were scores of cats, most of them feral, a few tame enough for petting.

Amphibians and reptiles, especially snakes with sleek colorful bodies, fascinated me. In the process of capturing a snake, I'd put up with the tarry poop it ejected, accepting that my hands would smell like burnt rubber for several days for the thrill of keeping it in a makeshift terrarium I'd made out of an old fish tank.

I placed a small frog in the terrarium with the snake and watched the gross and bizarre scene as the snake slithered up to the frog, which remained very still. The snake opened its mouth and fastened onto the frog's backside. As it swallowed its prey, the snake stretched its mouth wider and wider until it became just a mouth with a long body.

The frog's eyes popped as it disappeared bit by bit until all I could see was the bulge of its body, expanding the snake's neck and looking like a huge abscess. The bulge gradually worked its way down the length of the reptile. Later the snake vomited up the skin, which I examined with equally intense interest.

I often ambled down to the high banks of the creek bed on my own, fascinated with the wide swath of water that cut through the earth. I slogged through some of the boggy natural pools, the mud sucking at my feet. If I squatted and plunged my hand into the water and muddy bottom, I could feel the lumpy bodies of bullfrogs resting there. Sometimes I'd yank out a frog and watch it blink its astonishment in the light of day. I thought these frogs were adorable, and I would kiss their clammy cold mouths before I put them back in the mud or stuffed them in my pocket to take home. In the spring when I swam in the creek, I could usually cup up a handful of tadpoles, the tiny creatures in various stages of development.

Once I caught some baby salmon and stuck them in a shallow, plastic, compartmentalized dish. When I returned to my room later, I found the fish had jumped free of their prison and dried up on the carpet.

I climbed trees to look at baby birds in various cycles of growth in their nests, knowing not to touch them, while the parent bird flew around in circles, shrieking its distress.

Sometimes I was lucky enough to discover a litter of kittens left by the mother, who was no doubt off hunting for their next meal. I would spend an hour or more petting and snuggling the kittens, returning again and again to see how well they had grown and thrived.

I also collected and studied bees, spiders, ants and other insects. I did not consider it boring to sit for long stretches of time watching a web being spun or ants in their endless toil, marching to and from their underground colony, collecting bits of leaves, food, larvae and other dead ants.

Potato bugs disgusted me, though. Large and ugly with their fat heads and abdomens, they seemed to come out only after a good rain and to me they were good for nothing other than getting themselves squashed underfoot into a disgusting mess. But that was not the worst of it. Out from their ejected insides would come stringy, wormy, black things that took on a life of their own, growing in size before my eyes. For some reason there always seemed to be plenty of massacred potato bugs oozing their guts before the entryway to our dining area. The sight of them never failed to ruin my appetite.

Wildlife abounded in the surrounding hills. Deer, squirrels, raccoons and opossums were the creatures we most commonly saw. One evening as I walked from the dining area back to my bunkhouse, I had a prickly sense of a presence near me that made my body hair stand on end. Several feet ahead of me in the inky darkness I barely made out the shape of something big, its eyes reflecting the faint light of the stars above. I stopped and stood still, straining to make out what was before me. The animal had not moved, and as my eyes began to adjust, I realized I was gazing at an enormous predatory cat.

Terrified, I remained frozen, holding my breath as I gazed into those penetrating, glowing orbs for what felt like long slow minutes. When the creature moved, terror streaked hot through my body, but swiftly and silently the cat turned and disappeared into the shadows of the trees, the cloak of night rendering it invisible.

I ran so fast and hard to my dorm that it seemed my heart might burst, and my lungs collapse. I didn't confide in anyone about my encounter that night. Over a period of days I wondered if I'd imagined it. Then I decided to ask some of the other kids if they knew anything about large cats on the property.

"Yeah," someone told me. "There's mountain lions."

Unsettled, I asked someone else about the possibility of mountain lions.

"Yes," came the answer, "but they're rare to see. Usually they stay farther up in the hills."

So I hadn't imagined it. Yet I told no one.

I FOUND the ginger-colored kittens while I was trekking through a field on my way to yet another abandoned building on the property where we kids sometimes played. This building had busted-out windows because some of the boys used the space as target practice, stoning bullfrogs they had captured. Often they missed their mark and broke the windowpanes instead, leaving large shards of glass intact within the frames. Likewise, some of the walls were splattered with frog guts from successful shots, the dismembered amphibian body parts and pieces of glass littering the floor under the windows.

Old furniture stacked in a disorganized fashion throughout the building made it hazardous to walk through. Once, when I'd been hanging out there with several girls, a giant velvety black moth flew in through one of the windows and attached itself to the neck of one of the girls. She beat at the thing with frantic hands, but it clung to her, unmoving with its enormous furry legs curled against her skin.

The rest of us tried to help her, but she would not keep still and hopped about until she fell over a stack of chairs and box springs, dislodging the moth, which glided aggressively toward the rest of us while we screamed and tried to shield our faces. It flew over my head and found its way back out through the window.

The ginger kittens I stumbled upon were hidden in a bramble of bushes not far from the building. I heard their mewing before I saw them, a mound of squirming little bodies under the protection of the scraggly branches. The mother was nowhere in sight, but that wasn't unusual. I'd come across kittens before, and if I came back to their hiding place often enough, eventually I'd see the mother.

These kittens were newly born. Their eyes hadn't opened yet. Their ears were still flat against their heads. I stayed for a while, watching them and then went on my way. I came back a few times, but never saw the mother. On one occasion I sat a little ways away and waited, hoping to see a mother cat, but I never did. I wondered how long they had been on their own.

Knowing they would starve to death, I gathered the babies, scooping them into my t-shirt, and went back to my dorm, where I ran into several other girls, who oohed and aahed over my find. Happy to commiserate with others, we immediately planned a feeding schedule. Within an hour we'd scrounged up some doll bottles and filled them with milk. Adapting instantly to our new mama roles, we snuggled their tiny bodies and fed them, watching their tiny pink tongues lap at the droplets of milk.

One of the girls had an end table with a small cabinet that the demonstrators never inspected because she usually kept nothing in it. The cabinet was big enough for two shoeboxes, in which the kittens lived when we were away from them. Over several days they finally opened their eyes, which seemed too big for their little, furry heads. They looked around in wonder.

We were all in love, naive to think we could keep five kittens hidden and quiet all the time. An older girl, Gretchen, soon learned of our secret pets from one of the younger girls. On the fourth day, Gretchen burst into my room, her gaze roaming my space.

"What do you want?" I asked.

Her nostrils flared as she focused her attention on me. "Did you actually bring kittens here?" she demanded.

"They would have died," I said. "Something happened to the mother. She never came around."

Gretchen crossed her arms, her lip curling up slightly. "Where are they?"

"In Jane's room."

Gretchen turned on her heel and I followed her, speaking to her back. "We're taking good care of them. We found a good way to feed them."

Gretchen didn't bother knocking on Jane's door, either, but instead flung it open and stood for some seconds, silently taking in the scene. Jane and several other younger girls held the kittens, feeding and playing with them.

"We're taking care of them," I said again, hoping Gretchen would calm down when she saw what a good job we were doing.

When she turned to face me, hatred glazed her blue eyes to a fine polished marble, the pupils inky pricks of black. "You stupid, stupid, little bitch. You're a liar and a baby snatcher!" Her meltdown rendered the other girls silent. She shoved me out of her way and marched back down the hallway.

"Here, put them back in the boxes," Jane said quietly, pulling the shoeboxes out of the cabinet.

The other children did as they were told, gently placing the cats in the boxes, but Gretchen was already back with a demonstrator, who strode into the room, her gaze sweeping over the cats in the shoeboxes.

"Where did these cats come from?" the demonstrator asked.

Gretchen pointed at me, her other hand on her hip.

I was beginning to hate Gretchen.

"Pet cats are not allowed," the demonstrator said. "You can't keep them." She did not elaborate, but instead left the room followed by Gretchen telling her the situation was my fault.

Other children who had overheard the exchange wandered into Jane's room to look at the kittens. "They're so cute," they said, their remarks laced with regret.

The small group of us who had been housing the kittens knew we were in some sort of trouble, and a pall settled over us while we petted the cats and wondered what would happen.

"No! Please don't!" It was Gretchen's voice. I'd been sitting on the end of Jane's bed, and I sat up straighter, bringing the cat in my hands instinctively toward my chest.

The demonstrator returned with Gretchen pleading and crying behind her. "Please don't! Please don't!"

"Take all of the cats, and go and meet Buddy outside," the demonstrator said blandly, ignoring Gretchen.

Each girl took a kitten, and we trailed behind the demonstrator and Gretchen, who had given up begging and just sobbed.

Buddy, our physical education teacher, stood outside the dorm with one of the boys who held a container of ammonia. "Okay, come with me," Buddy said.

There were five of us girls, each holding a cat. We followed Buddy to one of the public restroom facilities, which had several toilets in a row. When I saw what we were going to be made to do, I put my cat in my pocket. My heart beat with such force that it seemed to pulse into my hands.

The boy who had been picked to help with the morbid project unscrewed the container of ammonia and poured splashes into each of the toilet bowls.

"Okay," Buddy ordered. "One cat per bowl."

The girls began to scream, and I took a step back, scrunching my clothes to hide the lump of the cat sleeping in my pocket. I let my arms hang by my sides.

Buddy pried open each girl's fingers, wrestling the kittens from their grip. One by one the cats were handed to the boy whose chest rose and fell rapidly, his face unreadable as he dropped each baby into the ammonia water.

I watched their small bodies writhe until Buddy was standing over me. "That's all of them," I told him. "There were only four."

His gaze swept my body. Satisfied that I did not have a kitten, he sent us all outside. Trusting no one, I went to the Shed in search of a box, my hand inside my pocket curled around the sleeping cat. Willing myself not to cry, I searched the back kitchen area, pretending I had some business there. I found a medium-sized cardboard box, picked it up and took it back to my dorm, where I lined it with a blanket before I struck a path into the hills.

Once I felt that I had hiked far enough, I sat down in the grass and pulled the mewing cat from my pocket, snuggling it under my chin as hot tears gathered in my eyes and splashed down, dampening its fur.

"I'm sorry," I whispered into its warm little body.

Carefully I placed it into the box with the blanket, which I scrunched up for a nest.

Hoping for the best, I left it.

Later that evening the wind picked up, and to my horror rain began to pelt down onto the bunkhouse. The storm grew stronger, and I lay in bed sick with the thought of the kitten outside. During the night the wind howled and rain pummeled the building, at times with such force that it sounded as if it might break through the roof.

The next morning, instead of going to breakfast after inspection, I ran directly up the hill to where I had left the kitten. The box had blown on its side. The blanket was soggy in the flattened, wet grass. The kitten lay still next to the blanket, its fur matted and slick against its body. I squatted, scooping it up, and found it was still alive.

It mewed weakly in my hands as I blew warm air onto its cold little body and then slipped it under my shirt to transfer some of my body's warmth to it. For a long time I sat on the damp ground trying to come up with some kind of plan. In the end I knew I could do nothing. There was nowhere to keep it safely, no place where it wouldn't soon be discovered. I removed the kitten from my shirt and kissed its head. I had given it some warmth, and it was quiet.

Righting the box, I placed the cat inside it and walked away, not looking back.

CHAPTER TWENTY-THREE

A Secret Zoo

"HEY," Melissa said.

I lifted my chin. I'd been lounging against an apple tree in the small orchard next to our dorms, watching her head toward me. Tall for her age, she took long strides, her usual dreamy expression out of synch with her habitual swift gait. Mentally, she always seemed to be somewhere else, her brown bushy brows creased in thought.

She eyed me for a minute, then said, "I'm starting a secret club."

"Yeah?"

"It's for ugly girls. There's three of us so far, and I wanted to ask you to join. You're the ugliest one in the whole school, and I thought you should be in it."

There was no malice to her words, and I wasn't offended. I'd been told how ugly I was almost every day by one kid or another and had accepted it to be true. In my view, Melissa was stating a fact.

"Who's in it?" I asked.

"Me, Laurie and Lacy."

Lacy was a dour, heavyset girl, one of the few kids who had a weight problem despite the active lifestyle of Synanon. She could be a bit snippy, and I didn't particularly care to be around her, but the club idea intrigued me as did the fact that Laurie had said she'd join it. A lot of the kids had been starting clubs. One girl had started one called Butterballs, a group for kids who were struggling with their weight.

"We're going to have our own zoo," Melissa said.

"What kind of animals are you going to keep?" I asked.

"Some of us just got some baby chicks and a duckling and we were thinking of catching some cats and taming them." Her green eyes locked with mine. Now I knew why the club was a secret.

"If the demonstrators find out, they'll take them and kill them," I said.

"I know," Melissa said, "but they won't find out. We found a place that nobody knows about. That's where we'll keep all the animals." She waited, letting me mull it over.

"Okay," I said.

Melissa grinned, flashing her long sharp incisors, and slapped my back. "Thanks," she said. "I thought I could count on you. It wouldn't be right if you weren't in it. We're all picking code names. Laurie's going to be Spike. I'm Bear. Lacy's still deciding. I thought maybe you could be Foxy."

"Yeah, okay." My code name meant little to me.

Later that day the four of us met in Melissa's (Bear's) room to brainstorm about how we would start the zoo. We discovered that among us we owned six chickens, one duck and zero cats.

It was clear from the start that Bear was the leader. "We need to work on clearing the area and getting it ready for the animals," she said. "Me and Lacy can get a hold of some cages and a few shovels, maybe a hoe." She wrote this down in a notebook she had on her lap, then glanced at Lacy.

"We'll be in charge of that," Lacy said. "Spike, you're good at catching cats; let's capture three, maybe four of them."

"Where are you going to keep them?" I asked. "If they're wild, they'll just run away."

"We're going to get extra cages for the cats," Bear said. "Foxy, your job is to help Spike catch cats. We all need to pitch in some money for cat food too."

"We should buy the food before we catch the cats," Spike said.

"Yeah, you're right," Bear said.

"How are we going to get a bag of cat food on the bus without anyone noticing?" I asked. "They check everything."

Bear stared at her notepad. "We'll find a way to get around it."

Every so often we kids were taken on field trips to the Petaluma Public Library and the Alpha Beta, a supermarket. We always arrived in a yellow school bus, filling the store in our unisex outfits and military cuts, mostly unaware of the stares of other shoppers as we explored the aisles, looking for our favorite treats. When we boarded the bus to return home, we opened our bags for the driver to look inside for contraband items. Bulky cat food would definitely be a challenge.

We kept the meeting short, taking a walk afterward to the secret place where we planned to have our zoo. I was surprised at how close it was to the dorms. None of us had played in the area, even though it was just a short way along a foot trail that ran mostly level and culminated in a quick, easy climb over an embankment to our spot. A small hill sloped down to a narrow clearing bordered by a thicket on one side and inlet of stream on another. Charged with the excitement of our new club, we ran down the hill, laughing, and explored everything in the vicinity.

For the first few weeks we focused on preparing the area where the cages would be kept. Sticks, branches and leaves were cleared away, tarps erected and shelves made to keep supplies. Cages were set on the ground, layered with more tarps and old blankets that we brought out to line the bottoms. The tarps and the nearby thicket and overhanging trees would provide protection from the elements.

Finally the day arrived for us to move the first of the animals into their new homes. These were the chickens and duck. As their baby fluff was molting and adult feathers growing in, we thought they would have a better chance of survival outside. We housed several chickens to a cage. The duck had its own home.

Eager to see how our residents had fared during their first night in our zoo, we ventured out and were relieved to find them sleeping, the chickens nestled against one another and apparently contented, warm and dry.

With the next field trip to the supermarket some weeks away, we focused on the animals we already had secured, feeding them once or twice daily and occasionally releasing them from their cages to run about under our supervision. As the chickens and duck grew in size, they remained relatively tame. All of the chicks turned out to be hens. One all-white chicken that we named Vanilla would actually come when called and even climb into the lap of whoever had beckoned her, laying her head affectionately against that person's chest.

Every chance I had, I went off to our little zoo on my own or with another club member. We began taking the chickens and duck on walks through the thicket, a lush quiet world of overarching branches that provided natural tunnels. Red and yellow leaves in various stages of decomposition carpeted the ground. The air was heavy with the scent of damp earth. At times I imagined myself in an otherworldly realm like the characters in C. S. Lewis's *The Lion, the Witch and the Wardrobe*.

During these strolls our chickens usually ran off to scratch and peck at newly discovered, previously unharvested plots in their quests for bugs and worms. We didn't want them to wander out of sight, so we repeatedly rounded them up.

They weren't the most obliging when it came to doing what they were told, but the duck apparently understood what we were trying to do and took on the job of keeping the chickens in order by loudly squawking and running after stray hens, nipping at tail feathers and herding wayward strays back to the group. He took his responsibilities so seriously that we started calling him Sergeant Deedle.

A month into our project, the demonstrators announced that there would be a field trip to the library with a stopover at the supermarket. Over the weeks we had been saving our money and giving it to Bear. An emergency meeting was called for the four of us to work out a plan.

"Sometimes the doors to the bus are left open," Spike said. "We could put the cat food under a seat and then get off the bus before anyone else gets on."

"What if I sit at the back of the bus and open a window and one of you hands the food up to me?" Lacy suggested.

Bear sat chewing on her eraser. "We should put the food in other containers like cracker boxes. Dump out the plastic packages of crackers and pour the cat food in."

We agreed that that was the best idea and it was exactly what we did, buying an amount of cat food we roughly calculated as sufficient to last until the next supermarket outing.

Once we had the food, Spike and I were ready to capture the cats. We'd seen a young tabby hanging around the bushes along our walk from the dorms to the Shed. Though not as wild as some of the other feral cats, the tabby was still skittish.

Over the weekend we decided to catch the tabby. We saved bits of chicken in our napkins from lunch and shoved the greasy lumps of paper in our pockets. We gathered twine, a cardboard box and one of the metal cages from the zoo. Spike made a hole in the side of the cardboard box and tied the twine at that hole.

We deposited the bits of chicken on a somewhat protected area of dusty ground not too far out in the open and set the cardboard box on its side, near our bait. Satisfied with our preparations, we hid as best we could in the bushes, lying on our bellies a short distance from our trap for a good half hour until Spike gave me a little pinch. Something was stealthily creeping through the bushes next to us. A moment later we saw not the tabby we had been expecting, but a gray cat stretching its neck, sniffing at the air. We waited for what seemed like slow minutes before it finally crept inch by inch toward the meat.

Spike's fingers tightened on the string, her face and eyes firmly set in full concentration. The cat was now almost upon the chunks of chicken, its neck stretched as far as possible from the rest of its body. I'm not sure what caused it to look in our direction, but the wary gaze of the green eyes caught sight of us. The cat froze. After a long minute it sniffed at the meat again before it made up its mind to go for it. As soon as it was crouched over the chicken pieces, Spike pulled the string. The box slammed down. Silence followed, then one plaintive meow. We jumped up, excited to have our first catch.

"Okay, you lift the box," Spike ordered, "and I'll grab the cat and put it in the cage."

"Ready?" I asked.

Spike hovered over the box.

"Go!" she said.

As I lifted the box, her hand shot down, grabbing the cat by the scruff of its neck. The creature fairly exploded into a bristle of gray fur that stood erect all over its body, claws ejected from the padded feet, lips receded so far off the teeth that the cat looked like a face of fangs with popping eyes. It made loud hissing noises and tried to flip itself to get at Spike's face, but she managed to keep the writhing ball of fury at arms' length and shoved it in the cage.

I reached over and shut the door.

The cat flung itself against the bars, hissing and yowling. After a minute it went into shock, huddled at the center of the cage, panting out its fright.

Assured that the cat had spent itself, I carefully latched the door and threw a blanket over the cage so we could transport it without anyone seeing what we had. A few days later we caught the tabby and named him Tiger.

We kept the two cats in cages for a few weeks, their waste collected and emptied from bottom sliding trays while they watched us in stiff wide-eyed distrust. Gradually they became tame enough to sniff our fingers without recoiling when we opened their cages' doors to deposit food and water.

One day Bear decided we should leave the cage doors open, allowing the cats the option to explore. This turned out to be a slow process that required much sniffing and inspection of the open doorway. Little by little, they came out and explored the encampment. Any sudden movement from one of the hens or duck sent them darting back into the safety of their little jails.

Eventually the cats allowed us to pet them while they lay in a flattened position. Another few weeks and they were scampering about playfully, using the trees to sharpen their claws and following us when we took the fowl for a walk. After a few more weeks they were tame enough to sit in our laps and purr.

With four of us running our little zoo there was always someone there to take care of things. Our biggest concern was having enough cat food on hand. We never exactly knew when the next trip to the supermarket would happen, and when the food ran low we had to ration servings for every other day, reasoning that the cats could catch rats and mice as they had when they'd looked after themselves.

Bear decided to ask her mom, who didn't live in the commune and for some reason was allowed to visit on a regular basis, to buy cat food for us. I had accompanied Bear a few times on these parental visits. Her mother, who reminded me of Chrissy Hinds from The Pretenders, usually spent the first ten minutes or so of their time together pinning Bear against her car or a wall while she examined her face and squeezed at all her blackheads and whiteheads. The next time her mother came to visit, she brought two medium-sized bags of cat food concealed in a black rubbish bag.

I spent every spare moment at our zoo. In our secret spot there was no radio blasting games of people screaming at one another or capricious adults who could change the course of a child's day or week on a whim. There was only nature and the animals, and I sat easily for an hour or two at a stretch just watching them. The other girls felt the same way. We started to make plans to set up tents so we could sleep at the zoo on some weekends and to acquire a camping stove and canned food for our meals. The possibilities seemed limitless.

Spike caught another cat, a silver-colored kitten with a white underbelly and large blue eyes. We couldn't wait to tame her so we all could begin holding and petting her. We called her Misty.

We had created our own little world and we managed to keep it secret. One afternoon I lay stretched out on the grassy embankment in the noonday sun next to Bear. Sergeant Deedle fluffed his feathers in the warm rays. The chickens pecked at the ground. Tiger raced halfway up a sapling.

"It's going to rain when Tiger dies," Bear said.

"What?" I turned to look at her.

She gazed toward the animals, but seemed as if she were looking through the scene.

"When Tiger dies, it's going to rain," she said.

I picked at some grass and tried to mentally brush off her comment. *Why did she have to ruin the mood? Say something so morbid? What was Bear talking about anyway?* I tried to focus on the animals, but couldn't. I turned on my belly, worry prickling its way through my thoughts.

"Why did you say that?" I asked.

Bear looked at me, her green eyes glazed. "Because it's true."

Our private world began to unravel when we added another club member and then two more turned up. Soon a small group of kids was privy to what we had built and wanted to participate. It all came crashing down when one of the boys, Donny, impressed with Spike's cat-catching skills, tried to catch a feral cat himself and the animal ripped apart his hand with its teeth. By then, some of the adults had gotten wind of our zoo, but were turning a blind eye. That all changed when Donny had to go to the doctor for stitches. It came out in the games that we were catching cats and keeping them as pets and that not only had Donny tried unsuccessfully to catch a cat, but a few of the other boys had done so as well.

Someone could get seriously hurt; wild animals sometimes carried rabies, we were told.

Immediate action had to be taken.

"Kill the cats, all of them," one of the demonstrators ordered.

Again this job fell to Buddy and a few of the other young men.

Mayhem broke out among us children as we begged and cried for our cats' lives to be spared. Some of us appealed to logic, asking about Orangie, a cat that had hung around the dorms for years and never bothered anyone.

The demonstrators herded us into our bunkhouses and

demanded that we stay inside. One of the newer club members had been bringing Misty around our dorms, and the kitten now sat on our back porch by the double glass doors, mewing plaintively.

I reached for the door handle as the first shots rang out, resulting in an uproar of sobbing and screaming from the children. One of the demonstrators grabbed my hand, pulling me away from the door. I ran to my room and threw myself on my bed, covering my head with my pillow to block out the sounds of the distant shots.

"Please let them get away!" I prayed out loud. "Don't cry, don't cry," I scolded myself and bit down on my fingers to distract my thoughts.

More shots.

It seemed to go on indefinitely.

The cats will be scared; they'll hide, I reasoned to myself.

Two hours later quiet returned, and we were given the all-clear. Children ran out of the dorms, dispersing every which way, seeking to know which animals had died and which had been spared.

As the afternoon faded to early evening, the temperature dropped and the air thickened with moisture that clung to our hair, giving us gray halos. The fog rolled in, unfolding eerie whitish curtains, obscuring our vision. I ran toward the zoo but had to stop because I could barely see two feet ahead. A clap of thunder exploded from the sky, followed by hard sheets of slanting, icy rain. I forged forward, my head ducked to avoid the cubes of ice that fell as if being hurled from above.

I heard kids calling out around me.

"I saw Orangie! He's alive. I found him hiding under the porch."

"Where is Blackie?"

"Did you see the white cat?"

I kept going. The fog thinned, moving rapidly. I broke into a run. At the upper end of the embankment trail leading to our zoo, Bear stood with something in her arms. I stopped then, and I knew as she made her way down, holding a small limp body, the brown and reddish patches of fur all too familiar. Closer still and I could see the perfect round hole a bullet had left in Tiger's side.

The zoo was over. And Bear was Melissa again, standing in the rain, her short hair plastered to her scalp, clothes clinging to her wet, cold skin, a dead cat draped over her arm.

CHAPTER TWENTY-FOUR

Books

"I HEAR YOU'RE A FAST READER."

I stood, hands folded before me in my schoolteacher's small office, avoiding her penetrating gaze. She was not particularly fond of me and seemed to bear me a grudge for reasons I never understood.

A few weeks earlier, I'd argued my case for moving up to the next grade level, but even though I'd completed all my work, she was determined to hold me back and have me repeat assignments for which I'd received sufficient marks. Outraged, I'd pulled folders of my schoolwork from her file drawer, loaded them on her desk and demanded that she take a look.

I didn't know whether she disliked the scene I'd made or worried that I might prove my point to someone else, but the next day, she ordered me to move my desk into the next room to join the rest of my peers who had moved up a grade some weeks ago.

"Some people say you can read a whole novel in a day," she said.

When I didn't respond, she opened a drawer in her desk and pulled out a small paperback. On the cover was a picture of a young girl with dark, curly hair standing on a hillside with a goat and snow-capped mountains behind her. She wore a cotton dress and smock of vest and apron.

"Have you ever read *Heidi*?" my teacher asked.

"No."

She lifted her chin and inclined her head toward a chair pushed up against the wall next to her desk. "Go and sit over there." She handed me the book. "I'm going to time you while you read. After an hour I want to see how far you've gotten and I will ask you questions about the story."

I sat down and opened the book, staring at the tiny print. No one had ever forced me to read, and I wasn't sure whether this book was the type of story I'd pick up myself.

I read the first sentence: "From the old and pleasantly situated village of Mayenfeld, a footpath winds through green and shady meadows to the foot of the mountains, which on this side look down from their stern and lofty heights upon the valley below."

My attention was already lost. I was not in the mood to read about the majestic beauty of the Swiss Alps or the next paragraph, which introduced a young girl and small child exerting themselves in climbing the mountain.

To tell the truth, I had been secretly making my way through Harold Robbins's *The Carpet Baggers* and *The Lonely Lady*, books I found around the property, in the dining hall and laundry room. In these stories I received my first taste of the seedier side of life: unscrupulous business practices; depressed, isolated women with suppressed sexual appetites; depraved men and their sexual fetishes; and cocktail parties where deals were discussed and feelings numbed through endless rounds of martinis and chain-smoked cigarettes. At the age of nine, the adult world of Synanon was shrouded in mystery for me. Harold Robbins's novels were like keys, which opened doors to secrets that I wanted to explore.

Heidi's cheeks, aglow with heat "the crimson color seen through the dark sunburnt skin," as the author described, did not compare to Jeri Lee in *The Lonely Lady*, which opened with Harold Robbins's protagonist forced to have an abortion due to the Rh factor of her blood. I didn't know what an Rh factor was, but I'd been immediately hooked.

Heidi's plight, also revealed on the first page, involved an older girl's dubious plan to deposit Heidi, who'd been placed in the girl's charge, at the top of the mountain with a relative known as the Alm-Uncle. While they walked through the little village of Dorfli, a place that seemed as interesting to me as the inside of a shoebox, various residents inquired as to the girl's destination, each expressing a sense of concern about the prospect of Heidi being left with the uncle. After twenty minutes I'd read only about three pages and could barely recall any of the story. I tried to speed-read, picking up bits and pieces of pertinent information, but was left with muddled images in no sequential order: wild flowers, a frowning uncle, fresh air, happy child.

The hour dripped by, and I jumped at the sound of a timer.

"How far have you read?"

I looked up at my teacher's flat face and down at the book in my lap. For the last thirty minutes I had been trying desperately to absorb the words. I had no idea where I was in the story because I'd skipped around in increasing panic. I chose a page at random and watched my teacher's lips tighten when she held out her hand for the book.

"Tell me what's been happening so far in the story," she said.

I stared at her, trying to think. I didn't know. I couldn't talk. I just stood there.

She set the book aside. "You have been fooling people into thinking that you're a reader. You are slow and have zero recall or comprehension of what you read." She opened a folder and made a note. "You can leave now."

I suppose my love of books began with my earliest memories of my mother reading *Goodnight Moon* to me. It began, "In the great green room there was a telephone and a red balloon and a picture of the cow jumping over the moon. And there were three little bears sitting on chairs and two little kittens and a pair of mittens and a little toy house and a young mouse and a comb and a brush and a bowl full of mush and a little old lady whispering, 'Hush.'"

My mother would place her finger over her lips when she said "Hush," her reenactment of the old woman sitting in the rocking chair.

Leaning against my mother's chest, I'd relax into our ritual of saying goodnight to each and every creature and object in the room.

"Your first word was 'book,'" Theresa had told me many times over the years. "I was talking to Grandma, and you were sitting on the floor and this little voice came out of nowhere and said, 'Book.' Grandma and I both stopped talking, and I said, 'Mama, did you say that?' She said no, and we looked at you, looking up at us. You were holding a book. You must have been about six or seven months, and I said, 'Celena, did you say 'Book'?

"You just kept looking at me with those big eyes. You had great big eyes like a Hindu baby. So I said, 'Celena, what's that? Is that a book? Book?' Then you said it again. The same little voice: 'Book.'" Theresa always told this story as if it had just happened the day before. She'd get worked up at the punchline, her eyes shining from the memory.

It seemed fitting that my first word had been "book" because books provided the ultimate escape from my anomalous environment. Other than an occasional field trip, usually to the supermarket or library, we children rarely left the Synanon properties. However, I found that I could go anywhere, whenever I liked, through books and later my own writings.

The shelves of the playrooms were well stocked with books for early readers up to young adult novels. Some of the picture books were typical for children. They included *Goodnight Moon* and *The Run Away Bunny,* both by Margaret Wise Brown, *Horton Hears a Who* and other books by Dr. Seuss, *Mother Goose Tales* and the like. Then there were the cartoonish informative guides to sex and puberty: *Where Did I Come From?* and *What's Happening To Me?* both by Peter Mayle.

Where Did I Come From? begins with the narrator announcing, "We wrote it because we thought you might like to know exactly where you came from, and how it all happened."

A few pages later, we see an illustration of a man and woman, the definitive parents, standing naked in a bathtub with bright cheerful smiles as the reader is taken on a tour of their reproductive anatomy and shown the distinct differences between them. This soon leads to the main action: Daddy, rosy-cheeked and on top of Mommy, enthusiastically pumping away. We had already been informed on the preceding page that when Mommy and Daddy are feeling loving, they like to kiss and then Daddy's penis grows big and hard in preparation for entering Mommy's vagina.

The narrator assures youthful readers that this sequence produces pleasurable sensations like a "tickle" in both partners. Daddy repeatedly rubs his penis inside Mommy until the sensation is so pleasant that something called semen spurts out into Mommy's vagina. The next page shows smiling sperm that look as if they might burst into song, swimming up a kind of tunnel that represents the inside of the woman.

The mission is successful for one of the tadpole-like contenders, and a sappy romance between the sperm and egg is played out in what looks like a sudden formal dinner party. The sperm has donned a top hat and sports a cane. He is in jolly suspended animation next to the egg, a blushing massive white blob of a thing with fake eyelashes. The two join forces, and voila! We have the beginnings of life. Also revealed are the biological processes of cell division and the progression through embryonic stages, fetal stages and finally birth.

What's Happening to Me? was just as fantastically detailed and riveting as its predecessor, chronicling the many biological changes of puberty. These books were well-thumbed and appreciated for providing many of us the opportunity to absorb this information privately. They were much preferred to the candid sexuality seminars we had been required to attend.

A book of photographs that made very little sense to me garnered more attention than Peter Mayle's books, which seemed tame in comparison. The photos were artistic-looking black-and-white pictures of naked children as young as five up to thirteen, with an adult or two included as well. One picture showed two young girls, perhaps twelve years old, with budding breasts, curled against each other in soft lighting, looking innocently up at the camera. Another picture showed a man laughing while holding a giggling young girl upside down, his limp penis drooped over her vagina. Another page displayed two naked girls, one spread-eagle under the other. The girl on top held a doll that she pretended to deliver from between the other girl's legs. These pictures were riveting and mildly alarming, giving a sense that something was about to happen that shouldn't.

When I wasn't marveling over Peter Mayle's rollicking, boisterous guides to puberty and sex or the erotic photography book, I was deeply involved in the timeless nursery rhymes and beautiful illustrations of Mother Goose or enthralled by the giant Walt

Disney book of fairy tale stories complete with colorful pictures from the beloved animated movies.

I frequently checked out the same stack of picture books from the Petaluma Public Library. At the age of seven, my favorite book was *Horton Hatches an Egg*, a story about a friendly elephant that's duped by a bird named Mazie into sitting on her nest all year long. Mazie tells Horton she will not be gone long, but instead she flies away to the tropics for a vacation, leaving poor Horton sitting indefinitely. Throughout this ordeal Horton is teased by a variety of animals and finally is kidnapped from his beloved home in Africa to brave a perilous ocean journey to the Americas, all while seated loyally on the nest, itself still cradled in a tree. All manner of questions were raised in my youthful imagination as I read this story over and over.

Why, for instance, did Horton never need to go to the bathroom or eat food? How did the men who found him manage to dig up the tree and transport Horton over a tall skinny hill that had a vertical incline of a sheer cliff and a peak so pointy and narrow that it looked like a needle? Why did the tree branch never break under Horton's enormous weight? I analyzed and picked apart my favorite story in the same way that I questioned my world and the nonsensical happenings at Synanon.

In the end Horton is accosted by Mazie when she happens to come flying by one day and sees him getting so much attention for sitting on her egg in a circus that he never wanted to be in. I always felt satisfied at the justice of the egg finally cracking open to birth a baby elephant with wings. This Dr. Seuss book, told in a humorous way that I could understand and to which I could relate at age seven, provided parallels to my own experiences and feelings of parental abandonment, displacement and living as an exile in a foreign culture.

One day an announcement was made, in typical Synanon fashion, that children seven and older were no longer allowed to check out picture books at the library and instead were required to borrow books with a minimum of one hundred pages. This rule felt like a disaster to me. I loved picture books. Books filled only with text were one step below newspapers, which at least had comic strips.

It took only a few days for me to realize that the new rule was one of the best ever enforced by the demonstrators. As I combed through the middle-school readers, I found Ruth Chew's quirky stories of children who discovered befuddled witches in their closets and under their beds. The cover image of two girls dancing gaily with a lion, a wreath of flowers around the cat's neck, soon had me immersed in the adventures of *The Lion, the Witch and the Wardrobe*. I inhaled the whole Wizard of Oz series and the adventures of Johnny Gruelle's Raggedy Ann and Andy.

Raggedy Ann was something of a mystic. She and Raggedy Andy were forever going on adventures in forests where hotdogs grew on trees, lollypop bushes abounded and there were soda water springs if ever anyone became thirsty. Usually the characters would stumble upon a general store in the middle of nowhere, the proprietor only too happy to give away his merchandise, as the dolls had no money. The suspenseful part of the tale came when Raggedy Ann and Andy were captured by a wizard or witch who lived in the "deep, deep woods" and wanted to cut Ann open and steal her magical candy heart.

Raggedy Ann's compassion for her wicked captors knew no bounds. In one story she chided Raggedy Andy for purposely distracting a witch who was trying to remember the spell to render Raggedy Ann unconscious so she could then destroy the doll. These villains always burst into tears of frustration when their spells didn't work, and Raggedy Ann would comfort them by telling them that all the magic they needed was right there inside of them and that if they would just clear the cobwebs of sorrow and selfishness from their minds, rays of goodness and kindliness would light up their souls. These enlightened words and a soft hug were all that was needed to forever transform the deranged creatures into beings of love and generosity.

After reading Raggedy Ann for a few years, I decided I wouldn't hit other kids unless they hit me first. I imagined Raggedy Ann somehow knew about this promise I made to myself and smiled up from the pages with approval.

I blew through the Ramona Quimby books and everything else written by Beverly Cleary. I strongly related to Judy Blume's coming-of-age stories, and *The Chronicles of Prydain*, a fantasy series by Lloyd Alexander, had me reading into the early-morning hours.

I also discovered Roald Dahl's stories featuring authoritarian schoolteachers and cruel caregivers and other books with similar antagonists, like the headmistress in *The Little Princess* by Frances Hodgson Burnett or Joan Aiken's *The Wolves of Willoughby Chase*. In these stories, little girl protagonists were kidnapped and shut away in a school run by mean-spirited women who forced them to keep their hair short. The children always escaped their circumstances and won out in the end. I read these books over and over.

It was, however, the Little House on the Prairie books in which, like the television show, I found the greatest parallels to my life. Living on a ranch easily lent itself to my imagining what Laura Ingalls Wilder's pioneer life had been like. In Synanon, adult members often hunted deer. The heads of the bucks with their crowns of antlers were saved and mounted on buildings all over the ranch property. The bike-shed walls were also lined with heads, their glass eyes glittering in the dim lighting.

In the Little House books, Pa kept a pig or two all year for slaughter in the fall, and Laura remembered with fondness being given the pig's bladder filled with air for use as a kind of balloon that she and her sister Mary played with. The pig's tail was roasted and given to the girls as a crackling treat.

Every year in Synanon we slaughtered our own pigs. Sitting on the fence of the corral, I watched as each got a bullet in its head, its neck slit and its body hung on a hook for bleeding and gutting. Later in the morning, we children were fed fresh sausages.

Laura Ingalls rode horses bareback with a cousin, galloping over the hills and through the meadows, the wind in her hair and a sense of freedom that thrilled me to imagine.

The commune kept horses, and learning to ride them was mandatory.

Laurie, who still went by the nickname "Spike," sometimes had the chore of searching for stray horses in the hills and bringing them back to the corral. After reading about Laura Ingalls's thrills of horseback riding, I asked Laurie if I could go with her one morning to scout out the horses.

"If you want," she'd said.

We woke at five on a Saturday morning and had a quick breakfast before we went to the tack room next to the horse stalls and collected a saddle, bit and straps. This equipment was for me. Spike rode bareback.

Into the hills we hiked with the gear and a small bucket of oats.

"They sometimes hang around this area," Spike said after we'd walked for close to an hour. "This area" was a vast stretch of land that appeared similar in every direction. Another hour would pass before we saw a band of horses off in the distance.

As we arrived, the creatures stood watching us, and I felt more and more uncomfortable with the prospect of Spike and me trying to persuade eight giant, muscular animals to return to the corral. Spike gave a low whistle, and one of the horses snorted, shaking its head and backing up.

"That's the leader," she said. "Come on, boy. I've got some oats for you."

The horse pulled its lips back from its thick, wide teeth and answered her with a high whinny.

Spike stepped forward.

The horse stepped back.

Spike set down the oats and grinned at me. "He wants them, but he knows it means he's going to the corral."

I wanted to go back to the property and forget the whole project.

Spike picked up the bucket. "We'll walk away a little and they'll follow."

Follow, they did. It was unnerving to have a herd of horses walking behind me and to have one of them nudging at my back.

Spike stopped and held out the bucket. When the lead horse stretched his neck and nibbled at the air, my friend reached out her hand and grazed his nose with her fingers. His head shot back and he snorted, showering my face with a fine spray of snot.

Spike laughed, unfazed by the fact that the whole lot of them could trample us to death if they didn't feel like coming back to the corral. "They know there's a lot more of these oats down below; they just don't want to be locked up to get them," she said.

Overcome by the temptation of the sweet-smelling oats, the lead horse took a few steps forward and dipped its head into the bucket, the force of its movement pushing Spike's small frame back. She petted his head while she attempted to remain standing.

"Here," she said to me. "You hold the bucket and I'll saddle him." Before I could say no, she pushed the oat bucket into my hands. Now I had to try to remain standing while the horse roughly satisfied his hunger.

Spike saddled him while a few other horses vied for the grain in my hand. Without fear, she pushed the other horses away, wrestled the grain bucket away from the lead, then coaxed him into accepting a bit and helped hoist me onto his back. Once I was astride, she handed me the grain bucket and climbed up behind me using the foot stirrup. From this position she was able to get another horse close enough to transfer herself to its back.

"Just give him a little kick; he knows where to go. The others will follow," she said.

I did as instructed.

My horse began to walk, but soon set off into a gallop with Spike riding alongside me. I thought of Laura Ingalls, riding free in the prairie lands a hundred years ago, as Spike and I smiled at each other and laughed at the exhilaration of moving at such speed atop these tremendously powerful creatures with nothing in sight except the hills of golden grass and blue sky above.

"WHAT THE CHILDREN NEED IS LOVE." These words were boldly stated by a short, slim woman who began to show up at the school on a regular basis. Her name was Pilar, and she was the mother of five children in the school.

Pilar was not like the other adults. She dressed all in black: black stretch pants, black Kung Fu jacket and black Chinese slippers. She showed up with a cloth bag full of massage equipment slung over her shoulder, herded any kids she could find into the Commons and told us to sit on the floor. Then she pulled out strange-looking contraptions. Into the hands of one child she placed a foot roller. Another received a neck roller. Still another got a giant vibrating massager. She then gave impromptu instructions, showing us how to use the equipment and pairing us up to massage each other's feet, neck and back.

I loved when Pilar came around. She was terrifically odd and apparently had some clout over the demonstrators, who listened to her when she gave suggestions.

Pilar's campaign to incorporate physical affection in the form of nurturing touch evolved into a twice-weekly bedtime routine of massage. Demonstrators on shift for the evening went from room to room offering a back massage or tickle before sleep. I'd always opt for the tickle, lying in bliss as fingers slowly and lightly ran over my skin for three to five minutes.

Pilar, I soon learned, was another close friend of Theresa's. One evening Pilar invited me to sleep over in her room, where we had tea and she asked me questions about the school and how I was getting along there. It was the first time since I'd come to Synanon that an adult other than Theresa took a genuine interest in me.

Later that evening, Pilar gave me two children's books. "This is a book about Frederick Douglass, and this one's about Harriett Tubman. Have you heard of them?"

I examined the cover of one of the books. A stern-faced black man, with a shock of white, cotton candy–textured hair in an old-fashioned dark suit, gazed back at me. The other cover depicted people huddled in the dark, apparently hiding out, escaping from somewhere. I'd never heard of either of them, I told Pilar.

Her slim, pale fingers traced the stern-looking man's face. "Frederick Douglass was a very important man in history. A long time ago, black people were slaves in this country and were owned by white people. Slaves had to work all the time and weren't allowed to learn to read or write. They had a very hard life. Frederick was born a slave, but he secretly learned to read and write and he escaped. When he was older he wrote about his experiences to help abolish slavery in America."

"What's 'abolish'?" I asked.

"To put an end to."

She pointed to the other book. "This is the life story of Harriet Tubman, who also was born a slave and escaped."

Escape. The word always caught my attention. The children

in *Hansel and Gretel* escaped the wicked witch's house after their father and stepmother abandoned them in a forest. The Little Match Girl escaped poverty through death and joined her grandmother in heaven.

"But Harriet did something different," Pilar said. "She returned to the plantations to help her friends and family escape from slavery, too. She also had others who worked with her. Some of them were white people who wanted slavery to end. They helped Harriet by hiding runaways in their homes as they traveled toward the Northern states, where black people were legally free." Pilar stretched out her hands. "The route they took, including the string of homes used as hiding places, was known by the slaves as 'The Underground Railroad.'"

I was enthralled and a little terrified. No one had ever told me about this history. I wanted to read the books right away. Questions raced through my mind: *When did all this take place? Was I in danger of becoming a slave at some point?*

"It is important to know your history," Pilar said, "and where you come from. When you understand history, you gain a better understanding of the world we currently live in and the people in it. A lot of us are fighting for justice in our own way."

When she finished talking, Pilar removed her black clothes, then put on a long, white cotton nightgown, knit cap and woolen socks. We climbed into her bed and I opened the first page of Harriet Tubman's story. I became absorbed in a world where people were owned like objects or ranch animals and were treated far worse. I read *The Underground Railroad* several times that night, as well as Frederick Douglass's story before I finally succumbed to the drowsiness that tugged at my eyes. Cuddling next to Pilar's warm body, I drifted off to sleep.

On our next trip to the Petaluma Public Library, I asked the librarian where I could find more books about Frederick Douglass and Harriet Tubman. I came away with *Narrative of the Life of Frederick Douglass, an American Slave.* Early in the book Douglass states that slave children from the area of his birth in Maryland were parted from their mothers as babies, then usually raised by an older slave woman. This separation of children from their parents reminded me of Synanon.

Harriet Tubman's life also brought to mind snippets of stories I had heard shared among the older children about another Underground Railroad, the one that provided an escape from Synanon. Somewhere nearby was a farm with a family who welcomed and hid runaways from the commune. Apparently there had been a number of instances in which teenagers, mostly from the punk squad, had tried to escape, but were caught, beaten, then thrown into a labor camp called the slug camp, where they worked long days at hard manual labor. I was not sure if any of these stories were true, but the escape stories of slaves had me pondering these rumors.

On the heels of my ninth year, I regularly read adult novels, and my fascination with American slavery led me to study other dark eras in history, such as the obliteration of Native American tribes in early American history, the German extermination of the Jews in World War II, and segregation and the Civil Rights Movement. I felt continually amazed at the atrocities people committed against one another and innocently assumed that all such cruelty had been left far behind us.

Reading about others' plights also helped me to put my own feelings and life into perspective. While I was able to draw some parallels between my life in Synanon and what others had endured, it dawned on me that throughout history people had lived through and survived exceedingly grave and often grim circumstances. This knowledge helped me to mentally devise a kind of pain quotient related to human hardship.

My Synanon experience could be considered hardly more than a bad cold in stark contrast to the experiences of those held in the harshness of the systemic crippling injustice of slavery. While I did not clearly conceptualize these ideas, my musings at nine years old were early sprouts of comprehension. A little Jewish girl in a Nazi concentration camp was fed only a bit of soup, if anything at all, on a daily basis, whereas I ate three meals a day. A slave girl could be sold and moved to a plantation far from her mother's location. I did not see my mother much; however, she still remained in my life. Weighing, comparing, contrasting and recognizing that others had survived far worse helped me to rise above my condition and concerns for myself on many occasions.

CHAPTER TWENTY-FIVE

Sugar Freaks

FROM MY DORM window I saw in the distance a crowd of kids from the school running at top speed in my direction. Some of them were jumping as if on springs, and I heard faint sounds of yelling. I opened the window just as one boy broke free of the group and sprinted ahead, whooping at the top of his lungs.

"What's going on?" I called down.

He kept running.

My two roommates, Becky and Emily, joined me, and the three of us stared at the fast-approaching mob of our peers.

"What's happening?" Emily asked me.

I shrugged and left the window with my roommates following closely behind. We walked out to the porch just as the fastest of the pack ran by. One of the kids shot a sideways glance at us and yelled hoarsely, "Sugar!"

Some of the kids were dancing and spinning; others skipped-ran.

"We can have sugar!" they cried.

I bolted down the porch steps into the rushing stream of children and caught hold of one of the boys.

"Is this true? It's not a joke?"

He grabbed my arms and began spinning me around, hugging me, then pushing me away.

"It's true! It's true!"

He continued to run, yelling out to any others who hadn't yet heard that the ban on sugar was over.

Joy.

Everywhere I looked were bright, beaming faces. I took the hands of one of the merry-makers and we erupted in laughter, breaking into a 1950s twist before spinning round, then running to catch up with the others and help spread the word.

Once we had gathered everyone, we turned and ran to the Shed. Pouring into the room, panting and talking over one another, we were shushed by some of the adults, who were listening with rapt attention to Chuck's gravelly voice on the Synanon radio.

"I just had a Snickers bar," he said, his voice blasting from the speakers. "And it tasted fucking great."

A roar of cheers erupted from the crowd of us gathered in the dining hall. Like a headline on a news syndicate, Chuck's announcement looped over and over along with VIP commentary about the Snickers incident and Chuck's decision to lift the sugar ban.

"He tasted a candy bar and decided it was really good!" one woman said as if she needed to say it aloud herself to be sure that it was true.

People patted each other on the back, hugged and laughed. Some of the men cleared away the tables and chairs. Someone turned on music. Inside of a minute we created the block formation for the hoopla dance. Clapping, dipping our torsos, swiveling our hips and spinning in unison, we laughed and cheered while we celebrated.

With the exception of the dinner party at my grandmother's and a brief Synanon holiday in Visalia, California, it had been a few years since I'd had any real sweets. Throughout the ban I had not lost my intense cravings for white sugar.

Before I arrived at Synanon, candy, colas, cookies and cake had been part of my regular diet as snacks and after every meal— so much so that I always felt thirsty because I rarely drank water. Whenever I asked for something to drink, someone handed me 7Up, Coca-Cola or Kool-Aid.

On the street where I lived with my uncle and aunt, an ice cream truck came rolling around in the late afternoon, with its colorful advertisements of chocolate-dipped ice cream cones and Hostess treats pasted on the body of the vehicle. The truck enjoyed a booming business, consistently swarmed by children and adults queuing up to buy the same items that were available in the market not far away. I usually bought either a Honeybunn, similar to a cinnamon roll without the cinnamon, or banana-flavored Now and Laters, hard, square, chewy candies that stuck to my teeth.

Theresa had been fond of the pink-and-white Mother's circus animal cookies, while my father was a fan of Winchell's Donuts. At Grandma Regina's there were usually homemade pies, cakes and cookies available at all times.

An absolute favorite of mine was a store-bought white birthday cake with fancy, swirly, multi-colored frosting. I missed this frosted cake so much that I sometimes drooled over a picture of a mandrill baboon in a wildlife book that I had in my possession because much of the animal's face was formed into colorful dips and ridges that reminded me of cake frosting.

In Synanon, we used saccharine in place of white sugar, despite the artificial sweetener's acrid aftertaste. When we weren't eating eggs and toast for breakfast, we often had Grape Nuts. Some of the children sprinkled their cereal with the powder from the pink packets placed in containers on the tables, but I ate mine plain. Nor did I touch the saccharin-laced birthday cakes. Gazing upon these cakes only depressed me. Despite their delectable appearance, they tasted the way I imagined cake batter would taste if powdered cleanser were added to it.

White sugar wasn't the only condiment omitted from our diet. At one point salt, too, had been prohibited and replaced with fake salt, which attacked my taste buds like a tangy Alka-Seltzer with the fizz factor dialed down. I stayed away from the stuff, and when my desire for salt became overpowering, I broke off chunks of the large salt licks attached to the corral fences for the cattle, though we kids had been forbidden from doing this and other children who'd had the same idea had been punished for it. When I was sure I was alone, I'd break off a piece of the salt and suck on it until I puked, and then I would suck some more.

With the ban on sugar lifted, adults immediately scheduled trips to the grocery store. Bags of doughnuts, Twinkies, cookies, cakes, chocolate bars and ice cream were purchased and handed freely to us children by the armload. Some of the kids who'd already made plans to leave the property for a brief trip into town collected money from the rest of us and made shopping lists of requested treats.

My first taste of sugar after years without it was not as great as I'd thought it would be. Though at first I was excited to receive an Oreo cookie, I could barely endure the first bite. It tasted terrible. How had I never noticed? The chocolate part was bad enough, but the icing inside tasted so sweet that I found it inedible. The fizzy lemon flavor of 7Up lingered on my tongue like watery, tangy pancake syrup.

A gulp of Coca-Cola created the sensation that my teeth were dissolving in the high carbonation. Alarmed, I ran to the bathroom, opened my mouth and saw to my relief that my teeth were still intact. Doughnuts still tasted okay and some cakes did, too, but only if they were plain, without icing or frosting. Gradually my palate adapted, and once again I built up a tolerance for sugary foods, though I still care little for soda.

The sudden release from years of sugar-deprivation seemed to turn the community into a horde of raving sugar lunatics. Everyone binged. Massive ice cream-eating contests became common. We'd file into the dining hall, where each person was given a giant wooden bowl large enough for four servings. We selected our flavors from five-gallon tubs, receiving two or more scoops of each flavor along with mounds of whipped cream, flavored syrups, nuts and maraschino cherries.

Walking back to my table, I carried a bowl of ice cream so large and heavy it could have easily satisfied a party of six. Yet these giant overindulgent servings were small in comparison with the bowls placed before the contestants, who sat on a makeshift stage. At the announcement of "Go!" they would tuck in, shoveling the cold treat into their mouths among cheers and whistles from the audience, many of whom attempted to keep pace with the contestants. I was not a big fan of ice cream, so after a few bites I left the rest to melt into a soupy brown liquid, mildly regretting the waste.

In Synanon we did everything in extremes. Disco parties were held often. Some began in the afternoon with a live production of early American Wild West culture. Dressed in our disco outfits of brightly colored polyester and Lycra spandex bell bottoms, skintight cat suits and miniskirts, with enormous platform shoes, we'd line up along the side of the road near the dining hall to watch the faux shootout. Groups of ten or twelve men dressed like vigilante cowboys from the 1800s would come galloping up on horses with holstered guns at their hips. They'd point their guns, which fired blanks, skyward, firing them off while whooping and pretending to assault one another. We stood clapping and cheering the showdown, which always ended in a duel. When one of the duelers inevitably received a mortal shot and fell to the ground, playing dead, the disco party started, with everyone rushing to the gambling rooms, which were open to all ages.

The main dining hall, reserved for dancing, was decked out with multiple strobe lights that flashed in rapid succession to long techno-disco songs, like Donna Summer's "I Feel Love." Our movements appeared as hallucinatory projections of patterns, shooting out every millisecond from the darkness to the machine-like beat and creating an ultra-hyped-up sensual feeling. At some point we'd form the block formation for the communal dance, the hoopla. Maybe a hundred people or more would perform the same movements in unison, a giant wave of bodies dancing as if one entity.

With the sugar ban lifted, these parties were supplied with vats of doughnuts, sodas and candy. In a mere three or four weeks, we began to realize we were eating ourselves sick. New rules were made to curb the abuse that we were doing to our bodies. Before long we were subject to spending limits on sugar: two dollars per week for the children. Sure, we balked some at the new rules. I must admit, though, that deep down I knew that the sugar limitation and its enforcement were for our own good.

CHAPTER TWENTY-SIX

The Case of the Rattlesnake

"A COUPLE of our members have run into some problems with the law. They've been set up."

I hugged my knees to my chest, trying to get comfortable in the impromptu meeting led by a man I didn't recognize. Some months shy of nine, I was mostly unaware of Synanon politics, as were most of the children my age, yet our ignorance hadn't stopped one of the demonstrators from plucking a handful of us out of our play, where we were herded into a smaller side room of the Shed. Inside, a few adults milled about with crossed arms and stern faces. I wondered if we were in some kind of trouble. As usual, I had no idea what I'd been dragged into until it started.

"Now, we can't stand for this," the man said. "There are journalists and newspapers printing all kinds of lies about who we are and what we do here. They're saying we're nothing but a kooky cult, and now there's this crazy lawyer telling the media that

Synanon tried to kill him by placing a rattlesnake in his mailbox. Can you believe that?"

The speaker didn't wait for an answer.

"We would never do that," he went on. "This lawyer put that snake in his own box and after he was bitten he yelled, 'Synanon got me!' How ridiculous! It was a complete setup."

The man paused, scanning the room. "Who here likes being in Synanon?" All hands shot up, including mine, although I still longed to leave.

The man's expression changed to grim satisfaction. "Joe Musico and Lance Kenton were accused. They've been set up and we've gotta fight to get them out of this mess."

My ears perked up. Joe and Lance? They were two of the nicest men I had ever known. Neither would ever do something like that! For once, I felt as indignant as the other community members.

A little over a year earlier, I had been invited, along with seven other kids, to spend the winter holiday at the Home Place, a Synanon property in Visalia, California. An invitation to the Home Place was considered a special honor. We spent four days in the VIP headquarters, where we were catered to and fussed over.

I'd had no idea what was happening when I'd boarded the Synanon jitney for Visalia or, when I'd arrived there, why I had earned the privilege to visit the special property; nonetheless, I had a blast. Although at the time we were not allowed sugar, this rule was temporarily suspended at the Home Place. We were treated to hot chocolate with whipped cream or marshmallows, ice cream and cider with cinnamon sticks, as well as enormous feasts of various kinds of meats, mashed potatoes, bread, rolls and pies.

In the evenings, we children in our pajamas and the adults in silk robes lounged on plush furniture in a massive living room before a blazing fireplace and watched movies. One that I recall was a dark comedy called *Who's Killing the Great Chefs of Europe?* about a psychopath who was systematically killing Europe's top chefs, the grisly murders themed to imitate each chef's most famous dish.

Our group leader for that holiday had been Lance, a young man who exuded Synanon wholesomeness. His hair clipped military style, his body strong and his smile wide, Lance displayed a constantly positive attitude. We played cards and board games together, or he'd hand out plastic squirt guns and we'd run around in a game of tag, shooting one another with water before darting off to hide. Throughout the visit Lance was full of ideas for fun activities, and Joe joined Lance and us in our games.

Like our properties in Marin, the Home Place was far removed from civilization. Snowy mountains hemmed the property, lending a hushed quiet to the outdoors. All of nature appeared to be asleep.

When Joe took us out to play in the snow one afternoon, I was more curious to explore the new environment, a blanket of white that stretched as far as I could see, than to hang out with him and the other children.

I wandered toward some spindly trees, trudging deeper into the drifts with every step until I managed to get myself stuck. I could neither lift my leg nor move it forward. Turning to look behind me, I saw everyone else at a distance. They were running after one another, throwing snowballs. Could they see me? I called out, but no one looked in my direction. Panicked, I tried to move my leg, but it wouldn't budge. What if they forgot about me and went back inside? I called out a second time, but I was too far away. The kids laughed and screamed so loudly that my shouts were drowned out.

I sat down and cried.

Minutes later I felt large hands slide under my arms, giving a quick tug and pulling me up out of the thick cold wet. Joe slung me over his shoulder, wading out of the deep snow as if he were walking through a mild stream of flowing water.

"It's okay," he said.

I rested my cheek on his shoulder, feeling instantly safe.

When I left the Home Place to return to Marin, I had only fond memories of both men. I just couldn't believe that they would try to murder someone.

We watched the recorded broadcast of Joe and Lance, surrounded by reporters, on the wall-mounted TV. An anchorman informed us that they were suspects in a conspiracy to murder an attorney named Paul Morantz, under the executive order of Chuck Dederich. We sat for a few hours, looking at other news clips and listening to various members speak their anger at the injustice being committed against us.

"We are the victims. We are the ones who are being attacked." The adults repeated this refrain over and over to us children.

The following year Joe and Lance were found guilty and sentenced to a year in prison. Still, I remained unconvinced of their guilt. Chuck escaped conviction, but was forced to step down as director of Synanon for several years.

The politics of the commune and its fight against "outsiders" resulted in a shift toward building power through us children. Boys were encouraged to learn how to shoot guns and maintain them. Some of our sports were substituted with karate, which Synanon called Syndo. The white uniforms were purchased and we were each given an outfit for lessons. We learned kicks, rolls and jabs and how to block an opponent. After karate class we stood in formation, enduring endless lectures on the physical excellence expected of us.

A black-belt guest teacher came to one of our karate classes to show us what we could achieve. A large beefy man with hair on his head that advertised his outsider status, he performed a demonstration in which he sliced a stack of bricks cleanly in half with the edge of one of his bare hands. A fine powdery residue of dust clouded the air and sifted slowly to settle on the table where the bricks rested.

His skills were impressive, yet the mandatory nature of the martial art instruction dampened my interest. Although I'd watched my share of Bruce Lee and Chuck Norris films, I didn't see myself becoming a master of karate or even accomplishing any level of competence.

As if to further highlight the truly quirky nature of the commune, we were also forced to watch the TV miniseries *Shogun,* all twelve dreary hours of it, while wearing our karate outfits and snacking on revolting, greasy, cinnamon-flavored crisps and apple juice.

By the time *Shogun* ended I had developed a deep dislike for karate and Japan. My dislike would persist for many years.

CHAPTER TWENTY-SEVEN

Lost

FOR YEARS I had a recurring dream in which I was a prima ballerina dancing majestically on stage before a large, adoring audience. I'd leap through the air, my legs spread in a grand jete, or I'd twirl in endless pirouettes and at the end of the performance the audience would throw flowers to me, their applause thunderous. Whenever I had one of these dreams, I'd talk to any demonstrator, who'd listen about the possibility of having ballet lessons in the school.

Therefore, I was pleasantly surprised when one day it was announced to me and a few other girls that we had been chosen to take ballet lessons in San Francisco. The lessons were to take place once a week on Mondays.

Since San Francisco was a good hour away, we had to wake up at four and be ready to board the 5 a.m. jitney that would take us to the Synanon property where our lessons would take place.

A massive structure encompassing a whole city block, the Synanon house of San Francisco had been obtained as a donation from the National Lead Company. It housed many residents and for a time was one of several main business hubs of the Synanon organization. Boasting a sweeping carpeted foyer, long narrow hallways and old rickety elevators that transferred residents between multiple floors, it was to us children a treasure trove of adventure and endless exploration.

On our first morning we were ushered into the dance room to meet our ballet teacher, a young woman with a quality of patience exhibited by very few of our Synanon demonstrators. The floor of the large room was carpeted instead of wooden; there was no barre and only a single rectangular mirror, propped against the wall. I was too excited about the lessons to care that it was not a real ballet room. Maybe the room would be altered later.

"I already know how to spin like a ballerina," I told our teacher as soon as our small group filed into the room. I followed my words with several turns, spinning as fast as I could.

"What do you think?" I asked, swaying slightly.

"Very good," she said.

The other girls silently absorbed this scene. I had no idea whether they wanted to learn ballet or not. Lacy and Melissa, my friends from the secret club, were among them. Lacy, tall and thick, and Melissa, even taller, were both aged twelve and unlikely candidates for a ballet class. But that didn't matter. Leaving the Walker Creek property once a week to come to San Francisco was more than reason enough for taking ballet lessons.

As the only animated student in the class, I inspired our teacher to begin our first lesson with learning to spot our turns. To demonstrate, she showed us how to prepare a turn. Placing one leg in the bent position of a plie and extending the other in front of her in a tendu, she held her arms in a similar fashion, one rounded in, the other extended to the side. "The trick is to find something across the room to focus on. With every turn, your eyes should always remain on your chosen object. Like this." She began a series of turns in perfect symmetry on the diagonal across the room, her movements so quick they were just a blur.

I was hooked.

The hour or so that we spent in class was over all too soon, but we were told that we had the rest of the day to do as we pleased, as the jitney would not be taking us back until late afternoon. So began a series of Mondays that we spent taking ballet lessons, eating what we liked, playing card games with some of the younger men who lived at the house and goofing off.

A month into our program we were granted permission to go out and explore the city and given pocket change for bus fare and a little extra to buy a treat or trinket. The only stipulation was that we had to return by 4 p.m. to catch the jitney back to Marin.

Melissa, Lacy and I hit the streets, basking in the rare warmth of a clear sunny San Francisco day. Strolling along the wide sidewalks, we gaped at the large, chunky buildings, some with fancy eaves and cornices, others brightly painted blue-and-pink Victorians. Like gawkers at a theme park, we viewed everyday pedestrians as exotic.

"We should go downtown," Lacy suggested. "There's probably a lot to do there."

We located a bus stop, hopped on the next bus that came along and got off when we arrived in what Lacy said must be downtown. Stores lined streets busy with tourists like us. For the next several hours we explored the shops. We found a music store with records and posters of our favorite rock musicians. Clothing and shoe stores carried the trendy Wrangler blue jeans, halter tops and platform shoes that we girls coveted. We wandered through an Indian shop that reeked of musky incense and sold colorful beaded jewelry and silk textiles fringed with tiny mirrors. The statues of elephants and four-armed deities displayed throughout the store reminded me of the pictures from the *Bhagavad Gita*.

At one point we stumbled upon a wig shop. The mannequin heads adorned with wigs presenting various styles in the window rendered the three of us temporarily speechless. Here was a store full of hair of every conceivable texture, style and length. Wigs were hard to come by in Synanon, as the long tresses were usually kept locked away with other theater props and brought out only for performances.

Traipsing through the store, I could hardly contain my excitement. We garnered curious stares from the employees and customers, but I didn't care. I was only nine and could still easily pass for a boy, but Lacy and Melissa had obvious breasts and feminine figures. Our boyish hair-cuts were the polar opposite of the long hair that women wore in the late 1970s. Even the men wore their hair long.

I passed one mannequin head after another, searching for the wig I wanted to try on, the one with the longest, straightest hair. Melissa put on a wig in the popular feathered hairstyle of the day and stood before one of the full-length mirrors, admiring herself. I spotted a foam head adorned with two long braids, a style I had often worn before coming to Synanon. I grabbed the wig, placed it on my head and then dashed to the closest mirror. A different child stared back at me. I looked like a girl, a real girl. I was even pretty. I couldn't believe it.

A saleswoman, who seemed to materialize out of nowhere, tapped me on the shoulder. "Excuse me. Where are your parents?"

I looked up at her.

She stood waiting with folded arms.

"I don't have any parents," I said. "I came here with my friends." I pointed to the hulkish form of Lacy still browsing the wigs and Melissa removing the feathered tresses from her own military cut.

"You're girls?" The saleswoman glanced at Lacy and Melissa again. "You are going to have to leave. You need to be here with an adult."

I didn't want to take off the wig. I glanced once more at myself in the mirror before I removed the hair and handed it to the woman, who took it from me. Her lips twisted as though she had tasted something sour as she returned the wig to the mannequin head.

We left the shop and continued our wanderings to the piers shrouded by hazy sea air. Hungry, we purchased corn dogs and big, soft, salty pretzels. After lunch we decided it was time to head back.

Lacy scratched her chin. "Do either of you know the way back? I wasn't paying attention to how we got here."

I shook my head, and we both turned to Melissa, whose green eyes clouded in thought. When we'd left the San Francisco house, we'd had no bus schedule or phone number. We hadn't bothered to check the name of the street, and no one had taken the time to make sure that we possessed this information. Like our weekends at home, our time was our own, and we could go where we liked with no supervision.

"No one remembers?" Lacy said.

"We'll head back to the downtown area and catch one of the buses. It should take us back to where we came from," Melissa said.

We walked briskly back to the street where all the shops were. It didn't seem as if we'd gone that far, but the bustling street on which we found ourselves wasn't the same street we'd strolled along earlier. As we looked for something familiar, it dawned on us that we didn't know the name of the street we'd been on before.

We turned around and went back to the piers. Throngs of people milled about. A group of Japanese tourists in brightly colored clothing held cameras and talked among themselves. When a red cable car pulled up in front of them, Melissa, Lacy and I ran to catch up and board the public transport with the tourists. Hanging on to the railings we scanned the seaside attractions, but again saw nothing familiar. When the cable car stopped, we got off.

"I don't think we came from this direction," Melissa said.

Two men brushed past us, holding hands. Lacy frowned, staring as they went by. We circled for a minute or two, not sure what to do. Then, down the street, I noticed a couple from the San Francisco house. They walked arm in arm, smiling and talking with each other. The three of us ran to catch up with them.

"Hey!" we yelled, waving our arms.

The couple stopped and waited.

"Man, are we glad to run into you," Melissa said. "We're lost and we don't know our way back to the house."

The woman's gaze flicked over us, a pinched look of irritation replacing her carefree smile. "We're having an afternoon off," she snapped. "It's not our job to look after you."

"Yes, but we're lost," I said. A fluttery panic rose up inside me.

"That's not our problem," the woman said. "Don't bother us anymore." With that, they walked away.

The three of us stood there, deflated, watching them walk down another street until they disappeared into the crowd.

"Come on," Lacy said. "We'll go back the way we came on that cable car. I think the house is in that direction."

An hour later we were no closer to our destination. We caught another bus and then got off, aimlessly walking the hilly streets, looking at the different buildings.

Another hour went by. The buildings looked rundown. The people wore shabbier clothes. Cars whizzed by. We pulled closer together when an emaciated man in greasy, ragged clothing staggered by, his red watery eyes fixated on us. On the other side of the street, two tough-looking men with bandannas on their heads strutted ahead of us. The neighborhood appeared more desolate than the streets near the pier.

Tired and grumpy, Lacy suddenly whipped around and ordered me to walk faster. The cold air stung my cheeks as an ashy twilight descended. Drivers turned on their headlights. I ducked my head, counting the wide cracks in the sidewalk to distract myself from the nagging thought that we might remain lost. What would we do now that it was almost night?

A horn blared, catching our attention, and a car pulled up alongside us just as we were about to round a corner. Three muscular black men with shiny bald heads sat in the vehicle grinning at us. Although their heads were shaved, we knew immediately that they were not from our community. They had a casual demeanor and exuded a kind of foreign vibe that all non-Synanon people exhibited. The passenger rolled down his window, and the driver leaned over to talk with us.

"Hey, aren't you Synanon kids?"

"Yes," Melissa said.

"What are you doing out here in the Tenderloin? Are you lost?"

"No," I said. We didn't know these men, and I thought it was stupid to confide in them. Although we had never had any training in Synanon about the possible dangers of interacting with strangers, my feelings and response rose from instinct.

"We are lost," Lacy corrected, glaring at me.

"Well, hop in," the driver said. "I know where the Synanon house is. I'll drop you kids off there."

Melissa and Lacy headed to the car, but I caught hold of

Melissa's arm. "We don't know them." I tried to keep my voice low so the men couldn't hear us. "He might be lying."

"Just a minute," Melissa said to the driver. She gestured to Lacy to come over to where we stood and we huddled together. "They seem nice," Melissa said. We glanced at the men, who were watching us.

"We've been lost for hours! Let's just we go with them," Lacy said. She gave me a hard look.

"If they kidnap us, we won't be able to get away," I argued, wondering how Melissa and Lacy could jump in a car with strangers just because they said they knew we were from Synanon. All three of us turned to look at the men again. The driver's smile grew wider and he waved us over. "I promise I'll take you kids right to your home."

"I'm going with them," Lacy said and went to the car. Melissa followed seconds behind her.

"No!" I called out.

Lacy came back to me, her irritation exploding into full anger. "If you don't come with us, then you can just stay here by yourself and find your own way back!"

I watched them get in the car. Night had crept up on us, and there was no one on the street, just the cars whizzing by on the road. The men in the car could kill us and no one would ever know, but if they all left, I'd be by myself on the street in the area the driver had called the Tenderloin.

"It's okay," the driver coaxed. "We won't hurt you. I'll take you right to your doorstep." Being left alone seemed even worse than getting into the car, and so after a minute of indecision, I climbed into the vehicle, squeezing in with everyone else. As we pulled away from the curb, I gripped the arm of the door.

It was not a long ride. Within ten minutes the driver had pulled up alongside a massive, but very familiar building.

"That's you, right?" he said, pointing at our San Francisco

headquarters. The other men laughed at our apparent relief. After thanking them, we got out of the car and I waved goodbye.

The driver yelled from his window, "I told you I'd get you home safe, Synanon kid." I watched the car speed off down the street, the red taillights winking in the night.

CHAPTER TWENTY-EIGHT

R^{ay}

MY EYES BLINKED open in surprised response to a hard poke in my chest. A demonstrator hunched over me, hissing for me to get up.

I could hardly think straight as I stumbled out of bed, still half asleep. My roommate and I were ushered roughly to the closet to grab our shoes and told not to bother changing out of our pajamas. Just barely getting my shoes on, I was prodded to the hallway and left to stand, cold and baffled, with some of the other children, who looked as sleepy and disoriented as I felt. The demonstrator went to the next bedroom.

"What's going on?" I whispered.

"We're going to the Shed," one of the girls said, keeping her voice low.

"Hurry up! Everyone out into the hallway!" I heard other

demonstrators calling from the various rooms. More girls came out, some with their eyes half closed, others complaining.

"Why do we have to get up? It's two in the fucking morning."

"What's wrong? What the hell happened this time?"

"Someone probably stole some money. We're probably all in trouble."

"I bet they're going to make us play the game all night."

I closed my eyes, exasperated at the idea of waking up at 2 a.m. to sit and scream at people when we all should be asleep.

"I hope we don't get our heads shaved again."

This last statement brought on a collective dismal silence.

After bustling through the hallway, we filed down the stairs and met up with the boys. A demonstrator opened the front door, and a cold gust of air washed over us, prickling my skin through the thin material of my pajamas. I followed the other children into the dark morning, no longer tired. More kids from other bunkhouses joined us and we fell into our usual social groups, conversing in low voices.

". . . can't find her." I strained to hear one of the older girls walking some feet ahead of me. "She ran away, I think."

Someone ran away? Who? I walked a little faster to fall in step behind Donna, the girl I had heard.

"Did they find her?" Donna's friend Janine asked.

Donna shrugged.

"Who ran away?" I asked.

Donna glanced over her shoulder. Seeing me, she made a face and picked up her speed to put some distance between us.

"It was Sara." Sophie sidled up to me. In the bouncing glow of the flashlights, I saw a smile straining to break forth on her lips, her round eyes jumpy with the excitement of the scandal. Though Sophie and I shared the position of school pariah, she always seemed to glean facts and gossip quicker than anyone else I knew.

"Did they find her?" I asked.

"I think so. But I hope not," she added quickly.

If Sara were still on the run, how far would she have gone by now? I imagined her walking in the hills, feeling her way in the dark through grass that was sometimes shoulder-height, stumbling on dips and crevices. Did she even know where she was going?

Three years older than me, Sara occupied a social position on the lower rung of the popular crowd and was especially good at making trouble for herself. She was usually beginning or finishing some punishment, amongst them an afternoon scrubbing pots in the kitchen or several days of the silent treatment. A latent rage bubbled just below the surface of her temperament. Her mother, who had left the commune when she was small, never came to see her. She'd been told that was because her mother didn't want her.

At one point Sara and some of her friends had started a gang, calling themselves The Baldies after a movie we had seen called *The Wanderers,* about an Italian gang in the Bronx during the 1960s. The imitation Baldies were mostly girls and a few boys who put Vaseline in their very short hair and slicked it back. They roamed as a pack during free time, practicing being surly and giving all of us "murder-ones," as we kids called their mean, slit-eyed look. They talked back to demonstrators and roughed up a few of the kids to engender fear.

The Baldies gang lasted a week or two until they were squashed by the real masters of intimidation, the Imperial Marines, a fascist Synanon youth group that was being trained as a kind of mafia-like entity, a burgeoning army for the holy war Chuck was threatening to wage against outsiders who caused problems for Synanon. In any case, The Baldies was a flash-in-the-pan manifestation of delinquent behavior.

As we approached the Shed, I noticed quite a few adults also making their way to the building. After depositing our shoes in the vestibule, we continued into the main part of the mammoth dining hall, squinting in the glare of fluorescent lights.

The demonstrators circulated among us. "Sit down," they hissed.

There was nowhere to sit other than on the floor, and kids who did not obey fast enough were shoved down. A frisson of hostility bristled from the older children, commingling with the swift, panicky submission of the younger ones. All of us wondered what we'd done wrong. Why were we being punished?

The adults sat around and above us in the chairs used at the dining tables. There must have been a hundred of them, and at that moment they did not look human. With their shaved heads, grim faces and hateful eyes, they were like a pack of robots. My gaze darted around the room, searching for Theresa, but I didn't see her.

"Are they all here?" one of the men asked.

It was then that I noticed Sara off in a far corner, squeezed among the adults. Someone grabbed her arm and yanked her to the middle of the room. She kept her gaze cast down toward the floor, her hands folded neatly in front of her. A deep blush scorched her neck and spread in an angry rush to her cheeks, smothering them in blotches.

Hushed conversations circulated among the adults before suddenly dying down. A quiver of energy snaked through us kids, drawing us closer together. From the recesses of the unlit part of the dining hall, a man strode toward the center of the room where Sara stood.

"How dare you try to run away from Synanon!" His words seemed to blast through her small form, but instead of being cowed, she lifted her head and I could see the disgust and defiance on her flushed face. Here was the truth that so many of us children felt, displayed clearly on her features.

Her accuser was not prepared for this small act of rebellion. He began to yell louder, pushing his face into hers. "Not only did you run away, but you inconvenienced everyone. We all had to stay up and look for you! We had to call your father from the ranch so that he could come over here and deal with you!"

Sara's eyes widened.

"Ray!"

Ray stepped out from the pack of angry, bitter adults. His hair, just growing in from a recent shaving, stood in little dark indignant spikes all over his head. His stubbly face carried a greenish hue under the lighting. His brown eyes squinted into a hatred that his daughter did not deserve. Like many of us, Ray still wore his pajamas. He practically ran up to Sara, carrying a grossly large wooden paddle.

"You've inconvenienced everyone! I was awakened in the middle of the night to drive all the way out here because of you! I'm fucking angry. Tonight, I'm ashamed that you're my daughter."

Sara's chin quivered, but her eyes never left Ray's face, as if she were trying to understand something once and for all. He grabbed her arm, almost pulling her off her feet and proceeded to beat her with the paddle. The force that he used would have knocked her to the ground if he hadn't been tightly grasping her arm beneath the shoulder. At first she did not cry. We heard only the loud thwacking sounds that echoed through the building.

All of us kids had received paddlings at one time or another. Once, I, along with a group of other children, had been required to witness Gloria's spanking. The demonstrator had stripped her of her pants and underwear, forced her to bend to the point where we could plainly see her vagina and beat her until she spurted pee.

Sara's lack of tears or cries encouraged her father to strike harder. Thwack! Her body flew forward with each hit of the paddle, forcing her to dance in place. When she still refused to make a sound, the blows came harder and faster. Finally, after what seemed like a full minute, she let out a small whimper. Ray gave one more final strike, and a guttural sound of anguish shot from her mouth as he let go of her arm and she fell to her knees.

Ray stood hunched, his chest heaving, his anger spent, the paddle hanging limply at his side. He scanned the faces around him, looking lost. One of the younger girls who sat next to me leaned in closer, her shoulder pressing mine as if I could protect her. The original announcer came forward and took the paddle from Ray's hand, patting his back before motioning for him to sit down.

"Stand up," he said to Sara.

She rose to her feet, her face absent of color, gaze darting about the room. The man smiled and lifted Sara's arm high as a statement for all of us to witness this official conquering of her spirit. A thunderous applause arose from the empty pit of silence, triumphant applause from the adults that grew louder and louder, followed by shrill whistles and whoops of approval that emanated from every corner. The man dropped Sara's hand, and her arm flopped to her side as, leering down at her, he joined in the boisterous celebration. "Long live Synanon!" the applause seemed to say. It died out as quickly as it had come.

"Let this be a warning," the man said. "Any of you thinking of running away, it will be worse the next time. This is nothing."

It was over.

We got up and filed out of the building. The adults, having made their point, allowed Sara to join the rest of us. She would be put on contract for a week at the very least. No one would be allowed to talk to her, and she would probably have to wear a sign that said "I'm an Ungrateful Asshole" while spending her time at the sink, washing pots all day.

She walked as if in a daze, tears falling uncontrollably down her face. It was her own father who had punished her. Even more disturbing to me, Ray had recently love-matched Theresa. At some point my mother and Andrew had separated, and Ray had stepped in as her new husband.

I first became aware of Sara's dad when he began popping in now and then at the school. He was a short man who always wore high-water overalls, the cuffs riding several inches above his sneakers. He liked to joke around with the kids, giving the boys wedgies and performing complicated handshakes that lasted as long as a minute, requiring turning in circles, blowing an imaginary substance off your palm and exclaiming "Pow!" at the end.

I didn't like him. I didn't like his strange high laugh, a jet of sound that shot from his lips like that of the animated Woody Woodpecker, punctuated by a sucking in of air. I didn't like the way his head swiveled all the way to the side of his body, his chin resting on his shoulder when he laughed or that his nose was so long he could shoot out his tongue and lick the tip of it. His beating Sara further soured my opinion of Ray.

I learned from gossip in the coming days (and years later from Sara herself) that when she decided to take a chance on running, she hoped to find the family that hid runaways, but like many of her schemes and plans, this one fell apart for reasons that were entirely preventable.

After the lights were out and her roommates asleep, she'd set about packing a small bag with a change of clothes and food she had hidden. Then for some inexplicable reason she went into her closet, ate her packed sandwich and fell asleep. When it was discovered during the nightly head count that her bed was empty, the demonstrator on duty checked the bathroom. No Sara. Other rooms were inspected. Maybe she had climbed into bed with another girl and fallen asleep. It soon became apparent that Sara was missing. The girls in her room were the first shaken awake and interrogated as to where she had gone. When they appeared only disoriented, more kids were awakened. Panicked, the demonstrator left the building to round up other adults to search. It was during all this mayhem that one of Sara's roommates found her sleeping soundly in the closet.

As we kids exited the Shed on the night of her botched escape and public humiliation, three of her friends tore away from the pack, each grabbing a part of her body and encircling her in a soothing hug, whispering words of comfort. The rest of us fell back, letting them walk ahead, Sara clinging to the girls' maternal warmth.

For the first time I truly felt I was in some sort of prison, leading me to wonder again as I had countless times in the past how long I'd be at Synanon. I thought about the family who helped Synanon runaways, the family Sara had planned to find. I imagined their house, a small cottage somewhere in the middle of the hills.

Watching Sara and the girls who embraced her gain more distance from the rest of us, I saw my stepsister in a new light. Regardless of her failure, she had had the courage to try to escape.

CHAPTER TWENTY-NINE

A Physical Education

"I WAS BORN DEAD," Tim told me for the tenth time.

"Yes, I know," I said. I watched him bend over his shoe, retying the lace, contentment settled on his sleepy features. Tim was new to the community, and every day we kids were required to divide our time into two-hour slots to act as a sort of babysitter for him. He took immense pride in the fact that he'd been technically born dead, a fact that seemed to explain his mental retardation.

Most of the adults humored him, holding out their hands to have him slap them five and often asking him how he liked living in Synanon. He always said, "It's super!" which elicited the expected response, "All right!" This exchange was repeated all day, and Tim never tired of it. The demonstrators put Tim in as many school activities as he could handle and physical education.

Physical education in the Synanon school had always been

rigorous. Like inspection, it was performed military-style, and unless you were seriously ill, there was no getting out of the drills we were put through. After countless sit-ups, leg lifts, pull-ups and pushups, we ran a mile and a half to three miles, five days a week, in all weather. We ran in hailstorms, the small lumps of ice pelting our faces and bodies, and we ran in hundred-degree weather. We ran up steep hills, down the highway and around an enormous track.

I always focused on my breath, ignoring side cramps and any other kind of bodily pain. "Keep going," I chanted to myself. When that failed to stimulate me, I switched to "You can do it!" forcing my mind to override my body's complaints.

I found the exercise easier when I knew how long I would be running than when we veered from familiar routes. I was fast, usually the first girl to finish behind the three fastest boys. Buddy normally ran alongside us, speeding up and slowing down, always watching for slackers. He did not tolerate slow runners, instead urging them to pick up the pace by barking in their ear and running on their heels. Anyone he caught walking was made to start over from the beginning.

After our runs we played an hour or two of sports. We played every sport: baseball, football, soccer, hockey, tennis, handball and others. There was a call to action that demanded the physical excellence Chuck spoke about in his manifesto on raising children: "They're going to know how to punch, too, they're going to know how to do what they're told, they won't be such sissies and babies. Their imprinting is changing completely. It just might be that we have a hell of a good thing going."

The child's age was hardly a consideration. Once, during a mandatory six-mile race through the hills, I found two small girls no more than five or six years of age huddled in the grass, crying. "Please help," they'd called out to me. "We're lost." Others had run past them without even a backward glance. I stopped and took their little hands in mine, urging them to keep going. It would not bode well for them if they didn't finish.

"Line up!" Buddy instructed us. "You know what to do. I don't want to see a single movement. You hear me?"

Within seconds we were standing in our usual formation: five rows, six to a row, shortest to tallest. We stood erect, arms straight at our sides, eyes forward, unblinking, barely breathing. The sun seared the tops of our heads. I could feel a dampness spreading along my hairline.

"All right, give me ten!"

I groaned inwardly, wondering who had moved. I shot down with everyone else, hands spread shoulder-width apart, legs close together for the first round of ten pushups. The dark asphalt gave off the smell of warm tar. The pushups were easy for me, but some of the kids struggled. We all had to rise and fall at the same time.

"One! Get those asses down. Two! Hold it together. You want to go for twenty? Three! We're going for twenty!" Next to me, one of the girls whose arms were too thin and underdeveloped for such grueling exercise, struggled with trembling muscles to keep herself balanced.

" Five! Hold! When I tell you not to move, you don't move! Is that understood?"

"Yes, Buddy!" we all cried in unison.

"What?"

"Yes, Buddy!" My gaze snaked to the trembling mass next to me. It seemed as if all the blood in her body had traveled to her face. She stared miserably at the ground, mouth agape as if she could suck up strength through the air.

"You!" Buddy stood over us. I could glimpse only his lower legs, knots of thick, ropy muscles. "Get up!"

The girl almost collapsed before she rose slowly to her feet.

"Go to the front," Buddy said. "I want fifteen more pushups from the rest of you."

I powered through and jumped to my feet, followed by the others, and took up my rigid soldier stance. My previous companion stood before us, rumpled and wan, a red splotch on each white cheek.

Buddy was a massive black man who stood six feet or taller. His muscles looked like lumps of sleek dark steel. His bald head shone under the penetrating afternoon sun. He marched up to the girl, hulking over her. The dark eyes in her thin face darted up to assess her situation. Just as quickly she looked back at the asphalt, her chest visibly rising and falling.

"You think you can just cop out here?" His voice was soft.

She shook her head.

"What?"

"No, Buddy."

"All right. Down. Give me twenty."

"I can't." The words were just a hiss of breath.

She didn't see it coming, but we did. His large hand connected hard with her thin chest. She flew back, landing on her bottom, the wind knocked out of her. She opened her mouth, but no sound came out.

"You want to play games?" Buddy said.

She shook her head, eyes watering.

"Is this a game?" Buddy called out to us.

"No!" we yelled in unison.

"Give me twenty!"

She rose to all fours, shaking, and managed to get into the pushup position, her middle sagging.

"Pull yourself up."

She did, her spaghetti arms trembling harder now as she attempted to make her first pushup. Creaking down, she collapsed, her body convulsing in sobs.

Buddy stood, his hands on his hips, eyes hooded. "Up!"

With an act of supreme will, she pushed herself back up.

"Down! That's two!"

Again she collapsed.

My neck felt stiff. My eyes strained from looking straight ahead.

Giving up on the girl, Buddy began to pace among our ranks. "This is Synanon. You are Synanon kids, and I'm going to whip your asses into shape. You hear me?"

"Yes, Buddy!"

"After our exercises, we will be running. There is no stopping. I catch someone walking, all of you will start again! Understand?"

"Yes, Buddy!"

I heard the hollow smacking sound of something like a watermelon hitting the ground hard. It wasn't a watermelon, but Tim's skull. In a fit of epilepsy, he had fallen straight back from his military stance. We broke ranks and ran over to him. He was out cold, his body stiff. We stood, watching him. No one, including Buddy, seemed to know what to do.

After some moments, Tim's eyes fluttered. His face scrunched up as he came to and registered the pain. "Uh, ungh," he cried.

Tim's epilepsy was one reason we kids were required to divide up our time with him. He needed to always have someone watching him. Yet no one had trained us on what to do when he had an epileptic episode. This major detail escaped the demonstrators in charge of his welfare.

Tim opened his eyes.

"You all right?" Buddy asked, a nervous smile flitting across his face.

Tim said nothing.

Buddy reached down to the boy, who stared silently up at all of us, tears sliding down his face. Buddy pulled him to his feet, guiding him to a shady place to sit.

The rest of us set off on our run.

From that day forward Tim did not participate in physical education. Then one day he vanished just as suddenly as he had arrived. It may have been weeks before we kids even noticed he was gone.

IN THE SPRING of 1980 Buddy Jones put together our first basketball team to play against schools outside Synanon. I signed up immediately, excited to learn the sport and get the chance to skip some of the game-playing that usually took place after physical education and before dinner.

I was one of two girls who registered for the team, and after a week, the second girl dropped out. Almost from the beginning I became obsessed with the sport, practicing whenever I had spare time. I loved dribbling the ball and trying to do what I considered fancy actions with it, like dribbling it around my body or through my legs and trying to run it up and down my arms like the Harlem Globetrotters.

I began to gain proficiency at dribbling and snatching the ball from an opposing player. Buddy assigned me the position of shooting guard because I could move the ball up and down the court with some competence and without losing it too often to an opposing team member. I was great at defense as well, but lousy at shooting and scoring as most of us were. I spent as much as an hour practicing shooting the ball at the basket from different positions and distances and while in motion. My teammates began to call me Swish, not because of skill, but because we'd seen a movie about a woman nicknamed Swish who'd disguised herself as a man to play on an all-male basketball team.

Some of the girls asked if they could be part of the team as cheerleaders. Their request was granted, and cheerleading outfits were ordered for them. In the fall we rode out in our jitney to challenge one of the local Marin County schools on the junior high school level.

A mere quarter of the way through the game, it was already clear that we stank. The team we played against was tight, the players seasoned. Their action sequences were well-planned, and they spotted many of our weaknesses right away. When I played against my own team, I found it easy to follow the ball and intercept a pass, but the team we played against was swift, the ball sometimes a streaking blur. I got confused, playing my position as shooting guard but then forgetting and reverting to the role of small forward, trying to do post-ups after catching the terrifying whizzing object, throwing it at the net almost without looking and missing every time as several large boys bore down on me.

"Frederick!" Buddy yelled, calling me by my last name from the sidelines amid the maniacal cheers of the Synanon cheerleaders in their shiny, purple, short-skirted uniforms. Our cheerleaders did not understand the game and burst out in disconcerting shrieks that spun the other team's heads as we ran up and down the court. Frustrated at our ineptitude, Buddy continuously swapped us, hoping someone would know what the hell they were doing.

We lost every game. We were obviously not the superior athletes that Synanon members boasted we were. In honor of our participation, one of the schools we'd played against kindly made certificates for each of us. Mine read "Mr. Frederick." Just like Swish in the movie, no one had guessed I was a girl. Buddy lost interest in the basketball team and it folded.

CHAPTER THIRTY

The Ranch

IN 1980, a change in living arrangements required that the Synanon school be moved from Walker Creek to the nearby Ranch property, which until then had been living quarters solely for adults. The adults were ordered to take up residence in Walker Creek. We made the switch in staggered shifts, and I happened to be in the first wave of children.

We found ourselves inhabiting half-empty buildings, having the run of the property, sparsely populated by the demonstrators and us. For the first time I was given a room that came as close to being my own space as I would ever have in Synanon. The room held two twin beds and a loft, which also had two twin beds. I was assigned to the loft and told that if I wanted to share it with another girl, I could. At ten years old, I had spent the last several years crammed into rooms with other girls, where every square inch was utilized. The long rectangular loft, with its sloping ceiling, Berber-carpeted floor and small slanted window, was a novelty. I had no desire to share it.

Because there were so few of us and we were cut off from the main body of the community, a few routines, such as mandatory inspections, began to fall away. Games were played less frequently, and at times we didn't have physical education. There were fewer seminars and school life became a loose assortment of academic activities. Often we filled out worksheets in the playroom and then lay about watching cultural and historical documentaries. These programs were all hosted by the same dreary man, who, in a voice little more stimulating than a speech synthesizer, stood in a suit and tie and spoke of long-ago dynasties and ancient artifacts. Lulled to sleep, I found myself startled awake by dramatic music as the camera zoomed in on what the producer obviously considered riveting imagery and then pulled back to the gray-faced man, who never so much as cracked a smile. We watched many of these programs, which frequently substituted for classroom learning.

Later, math lessons, taught by a new teacher, were added to the curriculum. Short and stocky, Alan sported an afternoon shadow of heavy stubble every day. He had a thick accent and for most of the class period we studied a map tacked to the wall. Our sole focus was two countries: Iran and Iraq. Colored bits of paper were thumbtacked to locales within those countries. The papers represented national flags and signified where the bulk of the fighting was taking place. Each day Alan explained with careful detail the present situation of the Iran-Iraq war. Whenever one country gained an advantage, he moved a few flags from the other country's map to the map of the temporary victor. "This is very important, very important," he always added.

As usual, I was confused. Apart from what seemed to be an endless war, I knew little about the history or culture of either country or how their war related to us. Our math teacher never offered us this information. In the last twenty minutes of each class, we were given basic math problems—addition, subtraction, long division and multiplication—to work on with calculators. Chuck had at some point denounced an education in math. Instead, he wanted us to learn how to use calculators because, as he liked to say, "that is the wave of the future." Why waste time solving problems with our minds when we had the advanced convenience of modern technology at hand to help us get things done faster and more accurately?

At another point there was a brief fascination with the abacus among the school administrators. A Chinese woman who'd been brought in as a guest to demonstrate how to use one stood with her beaded contraption opposite another adult with a calculator. A problem of long addition was written on the board and a timer set for a competition between the two. The young woman's slim fingers flew over the beads, moving them up and down the wooden rods attached to the wooden frame. She called out her answer before the timer buzzed and while the other contender was still entering numbers into his calculator. Moments later he called out the same answer. We students gave them a round of obligatory applause. The Chinese woman grinned, gripping the abacus to her chest.

Though I was amazed that she could compute so quickly with just some beads, I was even more fascinated with her figure. She was so thin that she looked like she had been modeled from a Gumby cutout. From every dimension she appeared alarmingly flat and her eyes stretched into such extreme slits that I wondered whether she could see at all.

Although Synanon had been ahead of its time in integrating blacks and whites, there were few, if any, Asian people in the commune. I had come to acquaint Japanese and Chinese people with martial arts films and B-rated Godzilla movies. The latter had dialogue dubbed into English and also featured other giant dinosaur-like creatures from the Triassic period that suddenly came to life, with their only apparent desire being to trample people and rip up high-rises while shrieking their fury.

The young woman with the abacus had a heavy accent, her words seemed swallowed back into her throat, consonants evaporating every so often, vowels blunt. Certain simple words were missing altogether. Although I had just watched her solve long division on an abacus so quickly she'd beaten someone with a calculator, I concluded she must be somewhat slow simply because she couldn't speak English properly.

My lack of contact with the outside world fostered other ignorant assumptions. For instance, I thought that all people in Africa still lived in ancient tribal bands and that people in some parts of England still traveled by horse and buggy and wore eighteenth-century clothes.

My view of American family life was similarly skewed. Although I had spent the first six years of my life living outside the commune and I had clear memories of that time and had watched TV shows epitomizing contemporary culture, I somehow conjured in my mind a 1950s dynamic of American nuclear family living.

In my imagination most women were housewives, creating domestic havens for their husbands and children, an idea I loved. I wanted nothing more than to live in a house with my mom, cooking alongside her and working on needlepoint projects during my free time. In my fantasy I was enrolled in a regular public school and had long, flowing hair. Synanon was a distant memory, a strange blip in the blissfully normal life that I imagined.

My Synanon education lacked in other ways as well. I had no sense of geography and didn't know where one country was in relation to another. I'm not sure I knew what a continent was, nor could I have pointed out California on a map had someone asked me to do so. I still struggled with telling time from a clock, and although I wrote and read incessantly, I had not learned even simple grammar. My ignorance of narration and punctuation in my writing led to pages of words all run together in one long, confusing string of events.

After another month or two, the next wave of children came to join us on the Ranch compound. Having grown accustomed to the smaller group, thoughts of my other peers had dissolved into the recesses of my mind. For the most part, I did not miss them. Yet when they arrived, the second group merged seamlessly with the first. Within a few days it was as if we had never been split.

One of the boys, Chris Waters, did not arrive with the second group, but showed up much later. Like the other children, I had not thought about him and was surprised when one day I stepped from the playroom and found him standing in the small courtyard between the play building and some of the dorms. He'd grown several inches and stood with his hands stuffed in his pockets. He seemed out of place.

"Where have you been?" I asked, realizing for the first time that he had not been part of our group for some months. It startled me that I'd forgotten him so easily, even though I had never really liked him. He'd been one of the kids who'd liked to taunt me, but the mischievousness that usually lurked in his blue eyes was absent, replaced by a solemn and shadowy stare.

"I was away," he said.

"Away where?"

"Shh." Chris grabbed my arm and pulled me farther from the entrance of the playroom. "I can't talk to you here. Walk with me."

I stumbled after him, bewildered.

His voice low, he said, "Some men came and took me just before the big move."

"What men?"

His lips thinned as I watched him struggle to explain. "There's a camp where they are keeping some kids from the punk squad. They sent me there. It's like a concentration camp or something."

"What?"

We walked faster, his words painting a disturbing story.

"I had to sleep in a tent and dig ditches. Every day they made me run for miles at gunpoint with some of the other boys. We weren't allowed to stop and rest. Buddy's in on it. It was him or one of the other men who'd drive a truck behind us, acting like they were going to run us over if we stopped."

"Why?" Even as I asked, I knew the question was futile. So many things that happened in Synanon seemed to just come out of the clear blue.

Chris shrugged. "They told me I was behaving like a punk and they were going to teach me a lesson."

He stopped and we stood looking at each other. "They would make me do pushups." Chris threw a furtive look over his shoulder. "When I couldn't do any more, they'd punch me in the stomach or kick me. There are older kids who want to escape, but we're all trapped here. Did you know that the entrances to the properties are manned by some of the Imperial Marines, with guns?"

"They said it was to keep us safe from outsiders that want to hurt us." Even as I spoke, I knew that it wasn't the truth.

Chris shook his head. "That's only part of it. It's also to keep people from running away."

His words churned sickeningly in my mind as I scanned the hills around us.

"They could come for any one of us," he continued, "and throw us into the slug camp. No one tells you anything. You don't know you're going to camp, and just like that you disappear."

Slug camp was a place for people Synanon members deemed

worthless: parasitic, lazy slugs who needed to be taught a lesson. In slug camp people worked long, grueling days exposed to the elements. At day's end they slept outside in flimsy tents. They were shunned by the rest of community until they proved themselves to be one hundred percent on board with whatever Synanon happened to be dishing out. I had always thought slug camp was for adults. I didn't know that kids in my peer group also went there.

Chris watched me, and when I looked up at his face, I realized that the boy he had been was no more. We were not far apart in age, but he seemed much older now.

"They're all bastards. You can't trust them," he said softly.

He walked on.

I didn't follow him.

Some weeks later Theresa arrived on the property with Gwyn. When we had some time to ourselves, I mentioned leaving the community.

Chris's story gnawed at me. Almost two years earlier the members of a community called The People's Temple had committed mass suicide in Guyana. Those who did not willing drink the poison-laced punch were forced to ingest it drink poison at gunpoint, more than nine hundred people died. I'd seen pictures in TIME magazine of their bodies, men, women, children and babies, laying side by side. Synanon had been on friendly terms with The People's Temple, donating whatever we didn't need or couldn't use to them. One woman who survived the massacre had come to Synanon. I wondered how she could be so trusting again.

I couldn't seem to get through to Theresa merely by begging her that we leave.

"Where would we go?" she always said. "It would be tough for us to be out on our own without Synanon."

"We could stay with relatives," I'd say.

At times, she'd smile and list all the things Synanon had to offer us: food, shelter, friends, freedom from worries of survival. At other times, she was quiet, serious and nervous in response to my badgering. Her gaze would dart around as she worried about who might be listening. Yet she always concluded by making some positive statements about Synanon. I felt exasperated by my inability to get through to her.

For the first time my adoration of Theresa began to develop cracks. At ten years old and approaching adolescence, I began to have a heightened awareness of my mother's flaws as if a highlighter had been taken to every perceived imperfection in her character. She began to bother me. She seemed too dreamy, inattentive. When I spoke to her, I often had to repeat myself because she rarely listened to what I said and would become confused, picking up only the latter portion of my communication, thereby compelling me to start over again. As a younger child, I hadn't noticed this quality of hers. Perhaps it hadn't mattered because small children have a natural ability toward a wandering mind.

Theresa kept a dream journal and liked to read to me about spiritual journeys she'd experienced in her sleep. Frankly, I found this practice to be slightly kooky. But what bothered me most was that she seemed content to remain in Synanon although it was becoming clearer to me through her work as a domestic and some snide remarks made by demonstrators and other kids that she garnered little respect. I wondered why and how she tolerated it.

Being a voracious reader, I had graduated to reading mostly adult novels. When Theresa discovered the books I had in my personal collection, she confiscated them. "You shouldn't be reading these sorts of books," she'd told me, scouring my shelf and pulling out almost every novel. "The demonstrators shouldn't allow you to read these kinds of novels. They have graphic adult content."

As I watched her walk away with a stack of my books in her

arms, a white-hot anger seared through me. *Who does she think she is?* I thought. She's not raising me. She's hardly even a mother.

Also annoying about her was the fact that she seemed gullible at times, that she was attracted to oddball people in the commune and that she loved Sophie, whom I simply couldn't stand. Sophie always lit up when she saw Theresa and treated her very much as a mother figure. Many years later I learned that Sophie had no parent in Synanon. She had been left as an orphan, but because most of us had so little contact with our moms and dads, Sophie's situation had not been apparent to me. Even if it had, it's doubtful I would have been empathetic to her plight at the time.

Theresa's marriage to Ray also put a damper on our visits. Sleepovers were eliminated because as a couple they had a room to themselves. This meant that we had little privacy in which to talk about our feelings as mother and daughter or merely to connect, without Gwyn or some other community member taking up Theresa's personal time and attention.

When I considered my future, it seemed hazy. I knew that one day soon I would be an adult, as the teen years were short in Synanon. I'd try to picture myself as a woman in the community, working somewhere; but doing what, I couldn't imagine.

How hard would it be for me to leave once I had the choice? Would I be able to survive on my own? These thoughts sometimes kept me from sleeping at night. I desperately wanted Theresa to take a stand for us, to tell Synanon goodbye. I'd imagine us moving back to Los Angeles, starting over. When I thought of my mom and me surviving as a team, I felt sure we could make it.

Her marriage never crossed my mind during my fantasies. The fact that she had a husband evoked no consideration, wasn't even an afterthought. Marriage meant little to me, just as Chuck had said years earlier in an interview in the *San Raphael Journal*, in which he'd suggested that divorce and remarriage was equivalent to "little more than changing one's clothes."

My own parents had never married, and Ray was Theresa's fourth husband. My mother's first marriage was to a man named Rodney. Their union had been brief, and Rodney was thrown out of the commune before I arrived. I don't think I quite grasped the fact that Theresa loved her current husband, Ray, or that he had much importance in her life as I had initially worried might be the case after the sordid demonstration with his daughter, Sara. I might have thought she would just acquire another husband once we were settled on the outside. In my mind, Ray belonged in Synanon, and leaving the community meant leaving him behind too. Other times I worried that my mother stayed because she was afraid she would not be allowed to leave.

Not only did I focus on Theresa's flaws, but I also began to observe the demonstrators in a much more cynical manner. Feeling less intimidated, I started to view their arbitrary rules and punishments with contempt.

Having resettled into our normal routines after the move, games increased to a daily event. To whip us back into shape, we were required to participate in a mini stew, a game of twenty-four hours' duration. The stew started after breakfast, and we were off to a fierce start of attacks and counterattacks, which frittered away into jealous squabbles between some of the girls about who had stolen whose friend. Next came talks between couples who wanted to break up, each person backed by his or her best friends.

"I don't want to go out with you!" one girl yelled at her boyfriend.

"Why?" he demanded.

She leaned forward, lips peeled away from her teeth. "Look, sucker, I never wanted to be your girlfriend in the first place."

This remark brought on a backlash from the humiliated boyfriend's friends.

"You fucking slut! He's glad to be rid of your stupid pussy. He was doing you a favor!"

"Yeah. You dumb bitch, you're too stupid to know what you have!"

"Oh, you think you're good with girls, asshole? Have you ever had a girlfriend, dick-face?"

The rest of us, who were a few years younger, sat out the amorous savagery, neither sufficiently experienced nor much caring to participate. Hours dragged by as the demonstrators took turns watching over us and encouraging us to keep going.

"Play! Keep playing! This is a stew."

By midnight some of the kids had nodded off, spent, with nothing more to say. At some point I also drifted off and awoke to a demonstrator vigorously shaking me. "It's not time to sleep! We're still playing. You must participate!" The penetrating glow of fluorescent light, stark and hellish, illuminated my droopy-eyed schoolmates. My eyes felt grainy and scratchy with sleep.

"Fuck. I'm tired," I muttered.

The demonstrator pushed her face close to mine. A black fury swirled in the depths of her eyes, the bags under them swollen to half-moons from lack of sleep.

"You wake up and play. Do you hear me?"

I sat up straighter, blinking rapidly. I didn't know what was going on. Someone talked about a roommate not keeping her side of the room tidy. The child being attacked stared with glazed eyes, expressionless. The rest of my circle was almost comatose.

"Hey, I'm talking to you, asshole!" an attacker shouted, trying to bring the level back up.

I rubbed at my eyes and looked at the girl on the hot seat, waiting for her reply. She hadn't moved or even blinked.

"Are you listening?" The demonstrator shook her. Eyes open, sleep had found her anyway.

She let out a low mournful whimper. "I want to go to bed. Oh, God, I want to go to bed."

"Shut up! We're in a stew. Carla said you aren't keeping your room tight."

Her mouth hung open, her eyes stayed glassy. "My room," she whispered, trying to follow.

Another kid jumped in to help steer things around, bring us back from the dead. "Your room? You're a pig! When I lived with you, I was always getting in trouble."

I blinked again. *Jesus.* My neck felt like it was going to snap off. *How many more hours till the sun came up?*

We played endlessly. Those who dozed were slapped awake.

"Play the game! Play the fucking game!"

Hallucinations of dark shapes clouded my vision. When I closed my eyes for a blessed moment of rest, an electric static raged behind my lids. We were finally sent to our beds at six in the morning, yet I couldn't sleep. I lay exhausted in my bed, my body humming and crackling, beyond fatigue.

DURING A ROUTINE BACK-TO-BASICS, I was assigned to help Theresa in the laundry room as well as babysit three three-year-olds. Back and forth I carted mounds of linens in a large, square-shaped laundry basket on wheels. I loaded the basket with dirty sheets and then piled the small children on top, pushing my heavy load to the laundry room, where Theresa continuously folded when she was not loading or unloading linens from the machines. The clean, expertly folded sheets went into large, white mesh laundry bags that were placed back into the cart, which I then wheeled, the children atop, to the various adult bunkhouses.

At one point when Theresa had to go somewhere, she asked whether I could watch Gwyn as well. Reluctantly, I agreed. It didn't take long before I became frustrated with Gwyn's slow walk. After my constant prodding for her to please walk a little faster, she stopped and stubbornly wouldn't budge.

"Let's go," I said. "I have things to do."

She refused to move. Instead her lips snaked into the side smile that I knew so well. It was the look of a certain willful mischievousness that overtook her normally bland expression, the same smile that rose crookedly on her narrow little face when she purposely knocked things over to make more work for Theresa.

Furious that I had to deal with her at all, I jabbed my finger at her face. "Listen, you fucking retard. You need to move now!"

In one moment she leered at me and in the next her mouth had clamped down on my finger. It happened so fast I had no time to react. She bit hard. I thought she might take my finger off. Terrified, I screamed and smacked at her forehead, which seemed harder than rock, while the three-year-olds gripped the edge of the laundry cart, their eyes wide. Another child who happened to walk by came to my rescue and pried Gwyn's jaws open so I could free my hand.

The following week Theresa again asked me to watch Gwyn for a few hours. I spent the time ignoring her, my attention absorbed in a book, while she amused herself, constrained to a large playpen of sorts. A truce of silence held between us.

Then, a powerful odor wafted through the room, a wet, sticky fart smell that prompted me to look up from my book. Gwyn had removed her pants and defecated on her mattress. She stood watching me, eyes glinting with challenge. Her bare legs were pale, thin and wiry. Between them, a surprising black bush of pubic hair announced burgeoning womanhood on Gwyn's more or less underdeveloped girlish body.

Not sure what to do, I stood up and yelled, "You know better than this! Now I need to put you in the bath!"

She stooped down, grabbed a handful of her shit and slowly

smeared it onto her face and hair, smiling her little crooked smile all the while.

I ran into the bathroom, where I stood trying to calm my spinning mind. *Make a bath, make a bath,* I gasped to myself. I turned on the tap and went back into the room. In the one minute I had walked away, Gwyn had spread feces everywhere, all over her body and along the railing of the enclosed area. It was streaked along the walls and embedded in some of the carpet.

I couldn't do or say anything but squeak with rage and disgust.

Fortunately, Theresa returned and took over the situation. While I watched her clean up Gwyn's mess and patiently escort the girl to a bath, a sour feeling washed over me. I desperately wanted to spend some time with just my mom, without Gwyn, Sophie or Ray, and yet at the same time I seethed with irritation toward Theresa.

"I had a dream about Gwyn," Theresa told me after she had Gwyn bathed and dressed in fresh clothes. "I dreamt of her life before this one. In her former life she was a wealthy, horribly bitter woman who had acted selfishly toward others, creating a lot of darkness in her spirit. I learned that she chose to come back this way. She's working out karmic debt."

I imagined a rail-thin aristocratic woman with long, sharp nails and a narrow, gaunt-looking face. Thinking about Gwyn's former life, I wondered about my own. Was I working out karma too?

As the lawsuits began to pile up against the community and we suffered from bad press, a frantic optimism swept through the cult. Pasted smiles and "act as if" attitudes were reinstated, partly as a way to shape up and show the outsiders who we were, but mostly to prove to ourselves that we were right and our way would prevail. One day the world would come to Synanon, and we would be ready.

There were more seminars about the greatness of the commune and all that it had to offer. "The outside world is depraved with its miserable values and shortsighted ways," demonstrators lectured. "You are lucky to get such a valuable education."

In one seminar a male demonstrator kicked things off by asking, "Who wants to leave Synanon?"

Those of us who raised our hands were weeded out and sent to sit on the other side of the room. For the next two hours we were calmly lectured on the merits of Synanon and Charles Dederich's vision, a warm smile injected here and there. After this longwinded psychological inoculation, we were again asked who wanted to leave. My hand was the only one that went up. I didn't know whether my peers gave up their ground simply to end the talky lecture, were too scared to show their opinions publicly again or had been inspired by the chatty informality of the speech, but I knew without a doubt that I wanted out.

Would they let me go if I became insistent enough? The demonstrator's smooth, persuasive voice became harsh and probing, but I waited it out. When my turn came to talk, I simply stated that Synanon was not for everyone and that it was never my choice to come in the first place. This time the other children and even some of the other earlier dissenters joined in the attacks. I remained stubbornly unconvinced and reiterated that I wanted to leave. The meeting ended late that night. I had not given in, a loss for the school.

I became more rebellious. Weeks after the propaganda seminar I got up without permission from a dinner that had suddenly turned into a silent meal, the environment menacing and demonstrators hawkishly watching us, a punishment that far exceeded the small infraction of several kids talking too loud outside the dining hall before meal time. Tired of it all, I simply walked out, ignoring one of the demonstrators who yelled after me, "Where are you going?" I walked back to my dorm and into my room, where I grabbed a novel and lay back on my bed to read. I stubbornly refused the command of one of the children sent to retrieve me.

A demonstrator came to my room, treading carefully. It was a curious matter that I wasn't intimidated. "Why did you leave the meal?" she asked.

"Because I've done nothing wrong, but I'm being punished anyway. I'm not going to sit in fear while I eat."

The demonstrator did not reply right away. I watched her thinking over what I'd said. My lack of fear and refusal to be the victim in their bullying behavior had interrupted the usual script.

"Some of you kids were screaming and being disruptive outside of the dining hall," she said.

"Yes," I replied, "but I wasn't one of them. Most of us were being quiet. It was just a few kids making all the noise, but we're all getting punished, having to sit like a bunch of criminals. I won't eat like that anymore."

The demonstrator tilted her head and then nodded. "You're right. We overreacted. I'm going to lift the ban. Come back to dinner."

Surprised by her acquiescence, I didn't move at first. She reached out and took my hand. "Come," she coaxed. "Let's go back to dinner."

IT WAS during a game that I finally reached my limit with the unbridled authority in the hands of immature adults. A demonstrator in her early twenties sat, smugly attacking my mother's character and intellect.

"Your mother is a stupid woman," she said with a smirk. "She is slow. Dimwitted, in fact. I doubt she could survive at all on her own. She needs Synanon, but Synanon doesn't need her."

The circle had grown quiet. No one backed the demonstrator's play. Her mean-spirited attack crossed an invisible boundary we children had with one another. It was an unspoken rule that we did not hammer at each other's parents. I stood up, leaving my chair and walked over to the demonstrator.

"You need to go back to your chair," she said, her gaze darting around the circle, looking for support. No one uttered a sound.

My hand closed into a fist, which I shoved toward her face. I imagined my knuckles pushing up hard into the soft underside of her chin. Her gaze stopped roaming, and her eyes locked with mine, her shame and guilt, the wrongness of her attack growing in her widening pupils. I wanted to crush her round, soft face.

"Say one more word about my mother," I threatened.

She said nothing.

"I don't care about the rules," I said, bringing up my fist so that it was inches under her chin. "You bring up my mother again and I'll hurt you," I hissed through gritted teeth. My throat felt swollen and it was hard for me to talk. I watched her swallow, a flush of red flaming her cheeks and shooting down her neck, but she remained silent. I left then, opening the door and slamming it behind me.

As I strode down the hallway, someone yelled, "Celena." I turned to see Charlie, my old tormenter, standing at the door. The usual malice wasn't there. Something had replaced it. Pity? I tucked my chin and walked on.

"She shouldn't have done that," Charlie called after me. "She had no right."

I picked up my pace. If I walked fast enough, maybe I could beat the tears.

In another game, much larger than the usual group of ten or twelve, thirty of us sat in a circle. Verbal attacks, swift and brutal, shifted like an ill wind in no particular order from one person to the next. When it was my turn to be in the hot seat, twenty-nine kids screamed at me. I didn't care. Instead, I went into observation mode, noticing everything in acute detail. Some kids perched at the edge of their seats, pointing accusingly at me; others pounded their fists into their palms; a few held tight to their chairs as if they might jettison away. Twenty-nine kids telling me what an asshole I was. Twenty-nine kids screaming for no good reason. I smiled at the absurdity. Then I began to laugh.

"Hey, shithead, we're talking to you."

This recrimination only made me laugh harder. My peers grew angrier. All at once they closed in like a cloud of hornets, but I couldn't stop laughing. The more they screamed their frustration and insults, the funnier it all was. My stomach muscles contracted, squeezing the breath out of me. I wanted to stop, but the laughter kept coming, the weight of the manic humor pressing on my chest. I slid down off my seat and tried weakly to push myself back. I rocked in silence; sound left me as I tried to suck in air. Looking up, I saw that some of the other kids had started to laugh too. The virulent humor produced a hard, discordant sound that erupted out of us in wads of spit bubbles and drool. The demonstrators didn't know what to make of it, but soon they caught the humor bug and laughed too. We laughed for several minutes straight.

The laughing game, recorded as all games were, was later broadcast on the Wire. Upper management liked the session so much it was played over and over again. Theresa received congratulation for having such a super kid who really knew how to play her game.

CHAPTER THIRTY-ONE

L eaving Synanon

SEVERAL YEARS earlier a squeeze had begun to push undesirable members out of Synanon. The squeeze consisted of a series of radical changes that included the forced vasectomies, mandatory abortions and changing partners. Chuck's ever-increasing demands that community members either consent to whatever he threw at them or "get the fuck out" had been a large part of why the population steadily dwindled.

Theresa's husband, Ray, lost status by the day. In 1978 he had been among a group of individuals sent to the slug camps. He'd toiled in the cold and wet of winter, performing required hard labor twelve to sixteen hours a day, then sleeping outside in a tent. His unsavory reputation for embracing metaphysical beliefs created a condition called a jacket. Once someone was labeled as in a jacket, it was difficult to get rid of the metaphorical constraints.

Having had a chronic asthmatic condition since childhood, Ray contracted pneumonia two weeks into his punishment. His illness led to his early release to receive medical treatment and rest in his bunkhouse.

Being with Theresa lowered his reputation further, and in the latter part of 1981, he and Theresa found themselves on a list of members who were being sent to work outside of the commune. All the money they earned was to be rolled back into the community as payment for letting them stay. Theresa, surprised to find herself on the list, as it mostly pertained to old-timers, wondered about her job caring for Gwyn. Nobody wanted the job, and Theresa thought her position granted her immunity from working on the outside.

Theresa and Ray also had been gamed aggressively for corrupting Melissa and me with their unacceptable and weird spiritual ideas when we spent an hour visiting with them in their bedroom.

In the commune, an adult's bedroom was akin to one's own small home. In Ray and Theresa's room, a low table stood in the corner as an altar. It displayed a small golden bell with intricate patterns, a book of prayers and chants arranged by color, and a wooden incense burner. The last held a burning stick of incense, the thin wisp of smoke filling the room with a musky, sweet fragrance. A framed drawing of a man with long blond hair and a smudge of red on his forehead decorated the wall above the altar. Ray served Melissa and me piping cups of hot Mu tea, a sweet herbal therapeutic Japanese tea with high notes of licorice and cinnamon.

"Who's that?" Melissa asked, pointing at the picture of the blond man.

Ray scratched his beard and pulled his feet over his thighs, unwinding the cross-legged position in which he sat on a hard round pillow. Melissa, Theresa and I sat on similar pillows.

"Maitreya," Ray said. "He is a being of light who carries the Christ energy. Actually, Maitreya was Jesus' guide."

Melissa shot me a snide smile, but Ray didn't notice. Warming to the topic, he said, "We're entering a new age, and soon Maitreya will appear to all of us to spread the message of love and light."

I listened politely, studying the picture. Maitreya looked exactly like Jesus, except for the red mark on his forehead, which reminded me of the Hindu pictures of enlightened beings in the *Bhagavad Gita*. At ten years old I reasoned to myself that Ray's story of Maitreya coming to enlighten humanity was unlikely.

"Whatever you are doing, wherever you are, he will appear before you to bring his message," Ray continued. "If you are watching TV, he will come through the channel to talk to you."

"Isn't that far out?" Theresa said.

I nodded while Melissa smirked at her tea.

"They're crazy," she said once we were outside their dorm. Because I admired Melissa, her words were cutting, and I felt a flash of shame. Later, she complained to one of the demonstrators about Theresa and Ray, saying that they were trying to push religion on us. Synanon did not tolerate religiosity. The only devotion Synanon members were allowed was devotion to Chuck. Melissa's complaint prompted another ban on my spending time with Theresa and discussion among the demonstrators about whether she and Ray were mentally fit enough for children to be around. An official complaint was made to management. Ray's things were confiscated, and he was sent to work camp for a week.

During the evening hours when Theresa and Ray were alone in their room, they began to discuss their growing dissatisfaction with Synanon and the possibility of leaving. To leave the community was an undertaking that seemed insurmountable to many of the residents. Living in such an insulated society for so many years and being told regularly that it would be almost impossible to survive outside of Synanon made many people afraid to leave. To leave meant severing ties with close friends and sometimes children if one parent left while the other stayed. There were also restrictions against taking money or items of value.

Synanon management purposely made leaving difficult, thereby quashing any incentive to start a new life and inciting fear of the world outside of Synanon . Management wanted community members to see leaving not as a positive beginning, but a punishment. Even with the squeeze, it was still hoped that the Synanite would make the right decision and do what was necessary to remain in the commune.

Ray and Theresa had had enough. They talked to each other about how disreputable Synanon had become in their eyes. While the majority of community members lived by strict rules of austerity, a select group of VIPs lived a different life at the Home Place in Visalia, a life of unbridled luxury, with gourmet meals, regular spa treatments and personal servants. Shocking pictures of Chuck, his wife, Ginny, and daughter Jady boozing it up on a beach in Italy circulated through the community. Many of the VIPs had stopped cutting their hair and sported longer tresses while the rest of us maintained the military hairstyles.

The rise in violence and Chuck's increasingly sordid demands upon community members finally pushed Ray and Theresa to admit, if just to themselves and each other, that Synanon had become corrupt. My mother also missed seeing me on a regular basis; she missed being a mom. I was growing up, and while she spent the majority of her time with Gwyn, she saw little of her own child.

A Sunday newspaper prompted Theresa and Ray to action when Ray discovered a small ad placed by a community called

University of the Trees in Santa Cruz, California. The ad stated that the community was looking for new members. Bolstered by this inkling of hope, a decision was reached.

"Congratulations. I just heard," one of my peers, Sue, said to me.

Her greeting stopped me in my tracks. "Congratulations for what?"

She scrutinized me, then her eyebrows shot up. "You mean you don't know?"

"Know what? What are you talking about?"

"You're leaving Synanon."

Her words seemed to hang in the air. Was she putting me on? We stood next to some picnic benches, which were semi-protected by a canopy of thick plastic. She leaned against one of the aluminum pillars, watching me, waiting for my reaction.

Leaving Synanon was a dream for most of us kids and had been a fervent wish of mine since my arrival. Many of us couldn't wait to get out of the place. Being told that you were leaving was akin to winning a million dollars in a lottery, it was that exciting.

Sue smiled so wide that her face looked like it might crack open.

"How do you know this?" I asked. My heart sped up, knocking wildly against my chest, but I still didn't trust her news.

"It's all over the place. Everyone's talking about it. You and Sara are leaving with your parents."

I took off at a sprint for my stepsister's room. She had moved to a cluster of smaller, wooden, cabin-like structures, each offering a rare private space and large enough for one or two residents. Many of the older kids lived there away from the larger dorms.

Sara's door stood open and I found her in the midst of packing, which consisted of grabbing whatever she saw and throwing it in a box. Several other boxes were already filled with her belongings. When I burst into her room, she glanced up and our eyes locked.

"It's true!" was all I could think to say.

Sara walked to me in two strides and grabbed my hands.

"We're leaving!" she said.

We threw back our heads and screamed. Then we laughed and screamed some more while we jumped around like kangaroos and then danced all over her room. I did not know what to do with myself. Hysteria, exultation poured from my lips and my limbs jerked and flapped every which way.

"Come on," Sara said. "I'm all packed. Let's pack your stuff." We jetted out of her door, sprinting all the way to the dorms. Once we arrived at my room, we realized that we had nothing in which to put my things.

"I'll get more boxes," Sara offered, darting back out while I dumped everything I owned on the floor and bed.

In less than an hour all my belongings were in the boxes that Sara brought back, but our packing was premature. We didn't leave that day nor the next. Instead our parents were stuck in games in which they were scolded, berated and denigrated for their plans to depart.

"Are you crazy?" their peers demanded. How could they leave Synanon for the outside world that offered nothing? Nobody cared about you on the outside, life was tough, it was hard to get by. In Synanon they had everything they needed. All their friends were here. Just what in the hell were they thinking, taking Sara and me out of such a fantastic school and exposing us to mainstream society? They were throwing their daughters to the wolves. As time wore on and our parents worked on trying to make arrangements for themselves, the games became more aggressive.

A week later, Sara and I listened, wordlessly, to one of the men from upper management yelling about our family on the Wire. "Theresa and Ray can get the fuck out! But Celena and Sara stay! They are Synanon kids and Synanon's going to fight to keep them."

CHAPTER THIRTY-TWO

Goodbye

IT HAD NEVER OCCURRED to me that Theresa might leave Synanon without me. As Sara and I waited to hear our fate, my morale plummeted. I unpacked some of my clothes, but three or four boxes, mostly of books and writings, remained stacked between the twin beds of my loft bedroom.

Following the announcement on the Wire, Theresa was nowhere to be seen. I could not imagine being in Synanon without her, never to see my mother again, never to rejoin the world to which I knew I belonged. Would I remain in Synanon forever?

The demonstrators, not sure what to do, let me keep my belongings packed, just in case. I walked over to Sara's cabin a few times every day to ask whether she knew anything I didn't. She had kept her stuff packed, too, but had no extra information.

After several days, she said, "We might have to stay."

"How do you know?" I asked. "Did you hear something?"

She shook her head. "It's just that it's been a while, and I'm guessing Ray and Theresa are probably going to cancel their plans, or maybe they'll get thrown out. I don't know. But I don't think they're going to let us go."

"But they're our parents."

Sara's dark eyes, ringed by a faint purplish shadow, met mine. Her face was pale and she looked like she hadn't slept in days. "So, it doesn't matter if they're our parents or not. They can keep us here if they want, and Ray and Theresa can't do anything about it."

After a few hours, I left her room and wandered in a daze to a nearby play area atop a knoll, where a rope swing hung from a sturdy branch of a large oak tree. It was in use and several kids waited their turn. I stood and watched as the girl on the swing, Erica, flew high, whooshed back and zipped forward again in a wide arc. As she flew forward, she yelled, "Go away, Celena! We don't want you here. We can't wait for you to leave."

The swing slowed, and another girl steadied Erica so she could jump off the seat. Erica was short for her age and had to stand on tiptoe to whisper into her friend's ear. They both laughed and looked at me. I walked back down the little hill and to the dorms.

At night I lay awake, my thoughts spinning. I tried to soothe myself with the idea that they couldn't really keep us. Then the soft whisper—*yes, they can*—would stir up the panic I was trying to keep in check. *I'll write to my dad*, I thought. *What can he do?* I asked myself. I'll find that farmer that helps runaways.

To the forefront of my mind appeared Chris Water's face: that strange pinched look he'd had, his eyes full of a seriousness that had never been part of his personality. There were older kids who wanted to escape, but we were all trapped here. *"Did you know that the entrances to the properties are manned by some of the Imperial Marines with guns?"* My skin felt icy numb as I remembered our conversation.

I shifted my pillow one way, moved it another. They could come for any one of us and throw us into the slug camps. *"No one tells you anything. You don't know you're going to camp, and just like that you disappear."* My mind wouldn't shut off. I couldn't sleep, so I stared at the slanted ceiling. I'd doze off a few hours before morning and wake up tired, moving through my routine like a zombie to get ready for inspection.

Ten days after the news that we were leaving had been broadcast, the dining hall's outdoor speakers crackled to life as another announcement came through the Wire: "Sara and Celena no longer belong to Theresa and Ray. They think they're going to take our kids. They've got another thing coming. Synanon will fight for them and they will lose. Don't fuck with us. You want to leave, leave. The kids stay."

The announcement played over and over. I went to Sara's room and we held hands, listening to the final decision yet again. She walked over to one of her boxes and kicked it hard. I went back to my dorm and unpacked the rest of my things. We were staying after all.

While Sara received sympathy for her plight from her peers, I found myself even more estranged from mine than I had been before. Over the years I'd accepted that I wasn't well liked, but now the bristling hostility that emanated from the other kids became especially hurtful in light of the situation. When it had appeared that I might be leaving Synanon, no party had been planned for my departure, and no one had seemed to care. The incident made me aware of how despised I really was. I also didn't know where Theresa and Ray were. They were suddenly nowhere to be found on the property. Had they already left?

I ignored the teasing about my moving debacle. Days went by, and I thought about how close I'd come to moving away from

Synanon, to finally living with my mother again. I imagined what our life could have been like had we gotten the chance to live in our own home like normal people. I'd have gone to a real school, and when school the day had ended, I'd have gone home, where Theresa would be waiting. She'd ask me how my day went and we'd eat dinner that she'd cooked. I thought about how irritated I'd been with Theresa lately and felt sorry that I'd wasted time feeling angry with her, not knowing that I'd probably never see her again. Other times I thought about myself as an adult with the right to leave if I wanted. Would I be able to survive on my own? For a long while I'd had the nagging suspicion that I wasn't learning anything of real value that would help me to survive as an adult without Synanon.

Almost two weeks passed before the next announcement broadcasted on the Wire: "Take them! Take your kids and get out!"

Several hours later, a demonstrator told me to pack my things. "You and Sara leave tomorrow morning."

I tried to keep my feelings in check as I reassembled the boxes and placed my things inside them. I hoped, really hoped, that this time it was true.

When Ray and Theresa were finally allowed contact with Sara and me, they told us that all the tough talk about keeping us in the commune was just hot air. With no parents staying behind, Synanon could not legally claim us.

Ray's ex-wife, Mary Ann, contacted her family in Santa Clara and asked if we might stay with them, explaining our situation. We could not stay with Ray's parents because they lived far away in Arizona, and his mother did not accept Ray's relationship with Theresa. She thought of my mother as nothing but a "quadroon," a disparaging term for a person who is one-quarter black by ancestry, and of me as "that dark girl."

Nor could we stay with my mother's parents because of old

issues she had with both of them. We had no money to speak of and nowhere to go. Sara, who had always been a good saver, offered her father a hundred dollars that she had tucked away, and Ray, unbeknownst to the other community members, possessed a handful of silver dollars. Mary Ann's family kindly agreed to take us in, and a little later my grandfather grudgingly gave Theresa a thousand dollars.

We left early one morning in late October 1981, two weeks after my eleventh birthday. The Synacruiser sat waiting for us, and we loaded our few belongings onto the bus before boarding ourselves. There was no one around to offer any goodbye.

Sara and I sat next to each other, staring quietly through the window at a pale, watery sky as the bus started up, yawning and creaking to life. Our vehicle moved forward slowly, crunching gravel as we edged down the road that wound its way through the property. The entrance gates stood open, flanked by armed men. Sara turned away from the window, a smile settling in her brown eyes. She took my hand, squeezing it, and we began to laugh.

Ray, his face thick with stubble, the skin stretched gaunt over sunken cheeks, eyes shadowed with dark circles from the tension of the past two weeks, hugged my mom, who nuzzled against his chest while he affectionately stroked her dark head.

"Goodbye, Synanon!" Sara sang out.

Yes. Goodbye.

A SHORT HISTORY OF SYNANON

In 1958 an old storefront in Ocean Park, California, on the Promenade was rented as a clubhouse for an unlikely group of members: The Tender Loving Care Club, later known as Synanon, specifically for people suffering from alcohol and drug addiction. Spearheaded by a dynamic and driven man named Charles Dederich, commonly known as Chuck, more than 25,000 people would filter through Synanon's doors over the commune's thirty-plus year life span.

During the cult's development, drug rehabilitation became just one of Synanon's many objectives as it expanded into building its own social and environmental awareness agenda through increasingly monitored and micromanaged lifestyle experimentation. Clean living, environmental consciousness, philosophical studies, interracial community and experimental childrearing were just some of the issues tackled both in theory and action. This "new" paradigm of collectivist and socialist structure attracted more than just dope fiends; college graduates, white-collar professionals, celebrities and wealthy donors also flocked to Synanon. These new members, called lifestylers, looked to Synanon as a kind of utopia. Synanon properties would grow to expand beyond Santa Monica, to Marin County, San Francisco, Oakland, and Visalia, California. There would also be property in Lake Havasu, Arizona, New York, and Berlin, Germany.

During the 1960s many social issues had come to a head: the civil rights movement, women's rights, environmental concerns, the Vietnam War, a rejection of orthodox religions and an embracing of Eastern spirituality, Buddhism, Hinduism, and Taoism. Conservatism was also sweeping the country, increasingly young adults were becoming polarized in their beliefs, some following the status quo, others questioning the norms of the day and demanding change. Communes were often attractive to people because they offered neatly packaged solutions to pressing social concerns.

Synanon was among a number of private communities birthed around this time. Chuck Dederick, being a fervent admirer of the philosopher Ralph Waldo Emerson and the psychologist Abraham Maslow, embraced Maslow's theory of psychological health and self-actualization and Emerson's philosophy on self-reliance. Chuck preached resourcefulness and independence, inspired by these two men and structured Synanon philosophy from the literary works of Maslow and Emerson while many of the unusual and bizarre actions taken by Synanon members were direct and unyielding dictates from Chuck as well. Throughout its lifespan, Synanon would be a dichotomy of self-actualization and mind control. People were encouraged to think for themselves and be innovative, yet never question Chuck, no matter how strange, disturbing or traumatizing to their lives some of his demands were. This schizophrenic mindset would create an emotional and psychological turmoil for many community members.

Over time, the organization grew corrupt and violent. Chuck, once a maverick for positive change, devolved into an egomaniac, wreaking havoc on his members' lives through unyielding commands often issued from his selfish whims. These dogmatic orders would have detrimental effects on Synanonites. Ultimately, the community would return full circle, residents succumbing to the abuse of alcohol and drugs that earlier members had once fought so doggedly to overcome.

Synanon fell to its demise in 1991. However, the approach of attack therapy such as The Game" and other abusive techniques established to control and straighten out the youth of Synanon are still in use in many troubled-teen programs that exist today. Some of these programs, such as Straight Inc. and The Seed, have been shut down by legal order after being subjected to lawsuits over various charges of mental, physical and emotional abuse. Although some scholarly studies have shown aggressive-style encounter groups to have an adverse psychological effect on participants, these tough-love teen programs continue to thrive and flourish. Maia Szalavitz speaks to this very issue in her book Help at any Cost: How the Troubled-Teen Industry Cons Parents and Hurts Kids (2006). She explores much of the background and history of the troubled-teen big-business phenomenon in America, discussing techniques used in some of these programs that stem directly from Synanon.

When the Synanon school began, the best and brightest teachers of the commune worked with the children; the intention was to inspire our capacity for innovative and philosophical thinking. Parents were regularly involved, and the school was often likened to Israel's kibbutzim (agricultural collectivist communities with socialistic economies). In a kibbutz, as in Synanon, children lived in separate houses and parents visited their children several hours each day. However, by the 1970s, kibbutzim were moving away from this model, and family members once again lived with one another. In Synanon, the opposite was true as the community became more antagonistic toward the traditional family structure.

Parents were expected to support this devolution in Synanon philosophy. They were ordered to spend less time at the school. Chuck and other VIPs who parroted his distorted opinions lectured parents about their involvement with their children, shaming moms in particular by calling them "soul-sucking" and detrimental to children's health. Parents were "gamed," i.e., screamed at by their peers, for such indiscretions as "poisoning" their children by taking too much interest in their welfare. Mothers deemed too maternal were called "head suckers."

By the time I arrived in February 1977, Synanon was at its most violent stage as a result of Chuck's growing paranoia of anything or anyone that wasn't part of Synanon. The fact that he had walled himself off in his self-created society, immune from any criticism from "his people," led him to become ever more delusional and Orwellian in his thoughts and ideas for what a Synanon lifestyle should be.

The school had devolved into an orphanage of sorts. Parents by then were encouraged to stay away and give up their children completely to the community. Amid the expensive lawsuits Synanon was fighting at the time, and due to the expense required to care for the children, Chuck began to view us as useless. Synanon children, Chuck complained, could not be put to work like the teenagers of the cult, yet we ate and took up space, contributing nothing of value while using community resources.

Instead of the best and brightest teachers, adults were sometimes assigned haphazardly to different positions in the school, teaching academic subjects in which they had no training. Rules and lessons were often random, incongruous with principles of developmental growth. The Synanon school's style was a paradox of militaristic rigidity and strict rules infused with intermittent periods of autonomy absent of adult oversight altogether.

For me, the "school" created a dissociative independent type of personality. To cope with the constant barrage of verbal attacks, whether directed at me, heard in passing, or on the Wire, the Synanon radio, I became adept at mentally detaching myself from my environment.

Despite Synanon's ambition to destroy the parent-child bond, my mother in bits and pieces, through letters and sometimes clandestine visits, communicated her affections to me, emotional inoculations that helped to foster a sense of strength and hope within myself that the cult could not conquer.

There has been quite a lot written about Synanon. They are memoirs, historical and philosophical literature, and scores of articles; however, the point of view is almost always from that of an adult who came to the community of his or her volition looking to escape the ills of modern American society. Of the children raised in Synanon, there is little written on what it was like for us growing up in the commune.

Here I offer my own story. I do not speak for all children raised in the community; this is a memoir of my journey. For the sake of privacy and respect for others, I have changed most of the names.

ACKNOWLEDGMENTS

First and foremost, I would like to thank my mother for helping me to tell this story. When I first began writing *Synanon Kid* in 2013, she generously spent many hours on the phone with me, answering all of my questions and sharing her perspective of our peculiar past. My children have all been wonderful in taking time to read several drafts and giving me valuable constructive criticism.

In 2014, I contacted Paul Morantz, the attorney who litigated Synanon on multiple counts and who Chuck Dederich attempted to murder by ordering two Synanon men to place a rattle snake in his mailbox. Paul has kept a dedicated blog of Synanon history and legal matters for many years, as well as writing two books on the cult: *Escape: My Lifelong War Against Cults*, which features Synanon among other organizations whose leaders turned malevolent and destructive toward their members, and *From Miracle to Madness*, a thorough anthology of Synanon history and a careful log of every legal issue Synanon ever had.

Paul was kind enough to have me over to his home and to read one of my earlier drafts over the course of an evening. He took notes, invited me back and sat with me for five hours telling me what he thought worked and what didn't. I am very grateful for Paul's honesty when he told me the manuscript still needed a lot of work. He was generous with his time and offered up the resources of his extensive library, which held a wealth of information about Synanon. I have found both of Paul's books and his blog a great resource of Synanon history. I have also supplied my memoir with facts from William Olin's memoir *Escape from Utopia: My Ten Years in Synanon* and David U. Gerstel's *Paradise Incorporated: Synanon—A Personal Account*, my mother's Kidsnatcher notebook and one of Chuck's manifestos, *On Rearing Children: From a Synanon School Health and Welfare Massive Dose.*

I would also like to thank the editors who worked on *Synanon Kid*. My friend Jeffrey Turnbull worked as a copy editor on earlier drafts, and Marion Roach helped with developmental edits. In later drafts, Marcie Geffner offered her expertise of developmental and copy edits, and my daughter Viva Wittman has also contributed to copy edits. Michael McConnel has done the final proofread.

I did not talk to anyone else who lived in Synanon, as I wanted to write from my own memories. I feel the recall of my own personal experiences and their lasting impressions lend an authenticity to my story that may have been muddled if I had collected my peers' perspectives and memories.

Finally, I am grateful for the serendipitous events that led me to visit the old Walker Creek property of Synanon in February 2017. My eldest daughter's boyfriend spoke to her of a beautiful piece of land in Petaluma where he liked to go hiking and mentioned that he would like to take her with him sometime to experience it for herself. When he described the place, she realized that the property sounded awfully similar to the Synanon property where I had grown up. Her boyfriend knew the caretaker of the property and after looking into it, informed my daughter that indeed it was. The caretaker, Patrick, and his wife, Melissa, graciously took me, three of my children and their significant others on a tour of the property. This was the first time I had been back since I was eleven years old. It was surreal, to say the least, and disorienting, as many of the buildings had been torn down and in some instances new buildings erected in place of the old. The property has been turned into an outdoor science camp for elementary school students and is also rented out as a conference center and for special events like weddings. There had been much rain over the past year, and the hills were a lush green, not the dry golden grass that I remembered. An old barn, which I thought might have once been the play barn in my youth, still stood. Inside it was much smaller than I had remembered, which is often the case with childhood memories of places. We spent a few hours trekking through the property and Patrick told me that every so often someone drives up claiming to have lived there as a kid when it was Synanon. Patrick said he usually takes them around and listens to their stories. One man once told him fondly, "We kids used to have the run of this place. We roamed where we liked. It was fantastic."

ABOUT THE AUTHOR

C.A. Wittman grew up in Northern California. In 1993 she moved to Maui Hawaii where she raised her children. *Synanon Kid* is her second book. Currently she resides in Los Angeles with her husband Frank.

Join my reading group at cawittman.com
cawittman.com
contact@cawittman.com

Made in the USA
San Bernardino, CA
19 August 2017